THE CRICKET BOOK FOR KIDS

THE HISTORY OF CRICKET, THE GREATEST PLAYERS OF ALL TIME, AMAZING GAMES, AND INCREDIBLE FACTS

LEONARD MATT

TOMOKAI RIVER

© Copyright 2024 Leonard Matt - All rights reserved.

The content contained within this book may not be reproduced, duplicated, or transmitted without direct written permission from the author or the publisher.

Under no circumstances will any blame or legal responsibility be held against the publisher, or author, for any damages, reparation, or monetary loss due to the information contained within this book. Either directly or indirectly.

Legal Notice

This book is copyright protected. This book is only for personal use. You cannot amend, distribute, sell, use, quote or paraphrase any part, or the content within this book, without the consent of the author or publisher.

Disclaimer Notice

Please note the information contained within this document is for educational and entertainment purposes only. All effort has been executed to present accurate, up to date, and reliable, complete information. No warranties of any kind are declared or implied. Readers acknowledge that the author is not engaging in the rendering of legal, financial, medical, or professional advice. The content within this book has been derived from various sources. Please consult a licensed professional before attempting any techniques outlined in this book.

By reading this document, the reader agrees that under no circumstances is the author responsible for any losses, direct or indirect, which are incurred as a result of the use of the information contained within this document, including, but not limited to, errors, omissions, or inaccuracies.

CONTENTS

Introduction   v

1. The History of Cricket   1
2. How Cricket is Played   13
3. The Best Cricket Players   21
   Garfield Sobers   23
   Rachael Heyhoe Flint   25
   Don Bradman   27
   Nat Sciver-Brunt   28
   Paul Collingwood   29
   Shaheen Afridi   30
   Ashleigh Gardener   31
   Sophie Ecclestone   32
   Suryakumar Yadav   33
   Rohit Sharma   34
   Brian Lara   37
   Smriti Mandhana   38
   Joe Root   39
   Kagiso Rabada   40
   Marizanne Kapp   41
   Babar Azam   43
   Hayley Matthews   45
   Jasprit Bumrah   46
   Chamari Athapaththu   47
   Shakib Al Hasan   48
   Laura Wolvaardt   50
   Rashid Khan   52
   Sophie Devine   53
   Ben Stokes   55
   Meg Lanning   57
   Kevin Pietersen   59
   Jos Buttler   61
   Sachin Tendulkar   65
   Kapil Dev   69

Imran Khan	71
Muttiah Muralitharan	75
Viv Richards	79
Shane Warne	83
Karen Rolton	85
Debbie Hockley	86
Eoin Morgan	88
Sarah Taylor	91
Lisa Sthalekar	95
Ian Botham	97
Wasim Akram	101
Richard Hadlee	103
Graham Gooch	104
4. The Most Amazing Games of Cricket	107
5. Incredible Facts about Cricket	127
Afterword	131

INTRODUCTION

Welcome to the wonderful world of cricket—a game of thrilling runs, spectacular catches, and fantastic finishes! Have you ever wondered how cricket began or who are the superstars of this splendid sport? If you're ready for an adventure through the green fields of cricket history and beyond, you've picked the right book!

Cricket isn't just a game; it's a global phenomenon that connects millions of fans and players around the world. This book is your ticket to uncovering all the secrets of cricket. You'll learn about how this game started hundreds of years ago and how it has evolved into the exciting sport we know today. Imagine playing a game that kings and soldiers enjoyed in the past—cricket is that game!

We'll dive into the rules that make cricket both intriguing and challenging. Don't worry if terms like 'wicket,' 'bowler,' and 'century' sound confusing now. By the time you finish this book, you'll not only understand these words, but you'll be using them like a true cricket fan!

INTRODUCTION

Ever heard of legends like Sachin Tendulkar or Vivian Richards? These heroes have made crowds cheer and opponents fear, and their stories are as inspiring as they are thrilling. You'll read about the greatest players who have ever stepped onto a cricket field and learn what makes them special.

But that's not all! We've also packed this book with jaw-dropping stories of the most amazing cricket matches ever played. Imagine a game so tense that it keeps everyone on the edge of their seats until the very last ball is bowled!

And for those who love fun facts and puzzles, get ready for cricket trivia and quizzes that will test your knowledge and tickle your brain.

So, grab your bat, or just your curiosity, and let's step onto the field to explore the fantastic world of cricket. Are you ready to become a cricket champion in knowledge? Let's go on this exciting journey together!

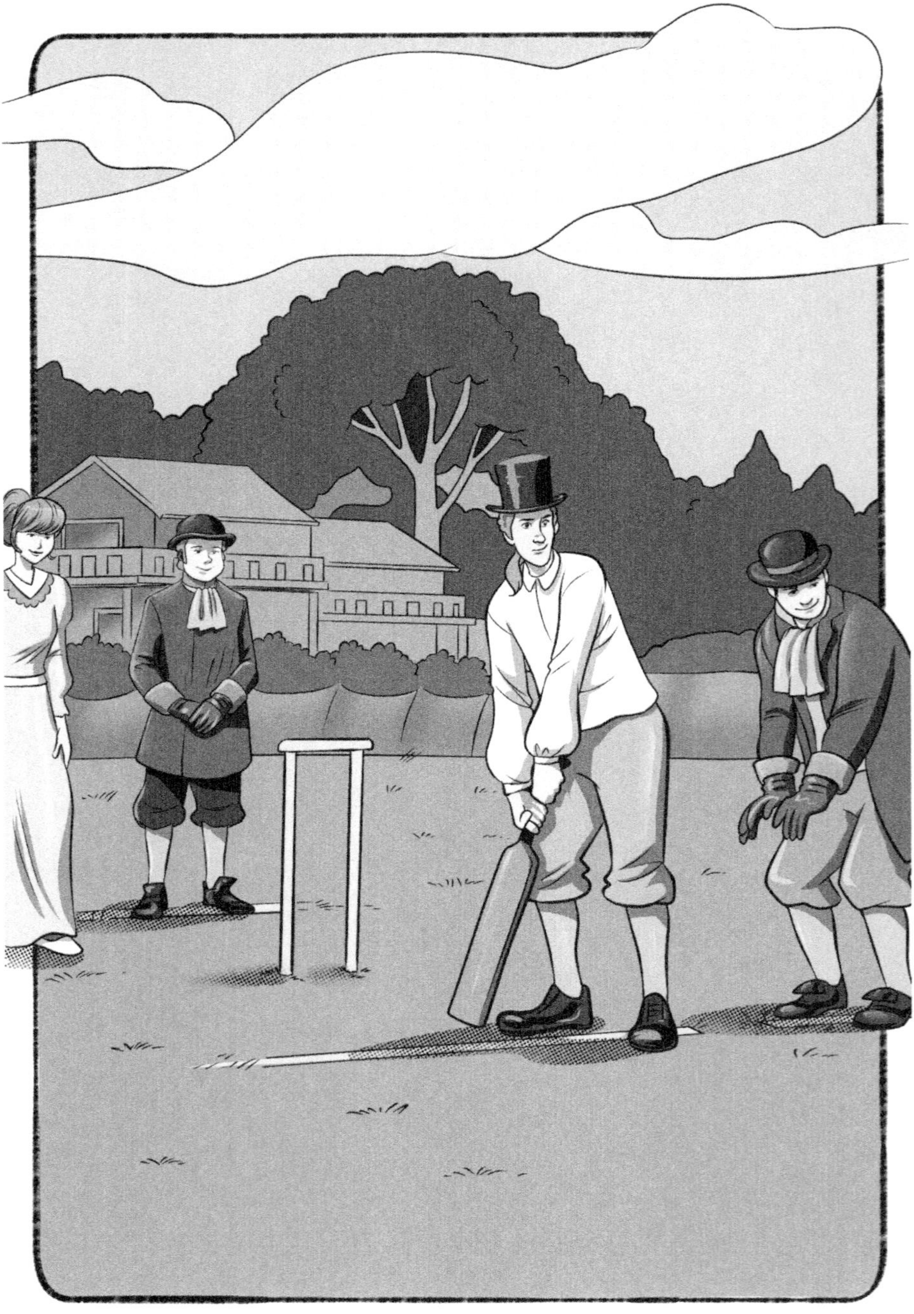

1

THE HISTORY OF CRICKET

Cricket is known as the Gentleman's Game and is watched and played by passionate fans around the world. It's called this because it's less flashy or show-like than other sports, like football or basketball. Cricket prides itself on intricate gameplay, skill and strategy.

In case you didn't know, the game is played with two teams. Each team takes a turn to bat and to bowl. The batting team must try to score 'runs'. These are like points. At the end of the game, the team with the most runs is the winner. While the batting team is trying to score, the bowling team is trying to stop the other team by knocking them out of the game, player by player.

The game is normally played on grass between two teams of 11 players, with a set of wickets and another wooden stick marker, a boundary play area, bats and balls. Two batters will take to the field, one at the wicket and another at the marker. The bowling team has one player bowl the ball while the rest of the team is fielding. The other players on the batting team wait at the sidelines for their turn to play.

The bowler will throw the ball toward the batter, and the batter will try to hit the ball with the cricket bat. If he hits it, he will run toward his teammate while his teammate runs the other way. If they successfully switch sides, that's one successful run. But batters can get automatic runs without even having to run. If they hit the ball so far it hits the boundaries, the batter will score four runs! Or if it goes really far, over and beyond the boundaries, that's six runs! That's called a maximum. And if the opposing bowler sends the ball high or wide of the batter's play area, this also awards the batter with an additional run.

On the other hand, if the fielders catch the ball straight after it's hit, that means the batter is 'caught out'. If the fielders catch the ball after it bounces on the ground, they can still get the batter out. They have to hit the wicket with the ball while the batters are still running. This is known as being 'run out'. Another common way a batter leaves the game is when the original bowled ball hits the wicket. This is called being 'bowled out'.

Players are also out if the ball touches their leg before it reaches the wicket. This is often called LBW (leg before wicket). Batters have to balance their game to score as many runs as they can while not being knocked out. One less common method is where a batter is 'stumped out'. This is when the batter misses the ball but the fielder behind (also called the wicket-keeper) catches it and makes it touch the wicket.

Once a batter is out, he is replaced by the next one waiting on the side-lines, and this goes on until all ten batting players are knocked out. Then the teams switch sides so the batting team are now fielding, and the fielding team is batting. After they've played and are all out, that's the end of the innings. After all innings are played, the highest run total of the two teams wins. We'll go into more detail about this as we continue to learn about this exciting game.

Millions and millions of people now know and love the game of cricket. It is often referred to as the second-most popular sport in the world, just behind football. Let's take a closer look at cricket's journey to becoming such a popular sport.

WHERE DID THE GAME ORIGINATE?

The origins of cricket can be traced back to the 16th century, when a historical record mentions 'creckett', which is believed to be how cricket was spelled back then. However, this was a very early form of the game. It was just a children's game, usually played alongside the game of bowls. Children used sheep's wool as a ball and a stick as a bat!

This soon became known as 'cricket', although the name itself is a bit of a puzzle to understand. While the sport is very much associated with England, the name might have been borrowed from the Dutch and French languages. 'Cricc' is a stick in Dutch and 'Criquet' means wooden post in French. Both relate to the game we know today.

People first played it with others in their local area. Areas like Yorkshire, Hampshire and Sussex here in England were the first to adopt cricket. In 1772, competitive cricket was born. The scores were officially recorded when the best players from Hampshire played a team from the rest of England. This started county competition between areas of England, as almost every area in the country had formed a cricket club by the start of the 19th century. In the beginning, it was very difficult for teams to play each other because they weren't close together. This changed when the railway network was built. The trains allowed teams from London to visit the North of England to play and made it possible for people to attend games played by their teams away from their home.

Cricket would soon become an international sport, with teams representing countries playing one another. While you would think England would be part of the first-ever international fixture, they weren't. In September 1844, the United States and Canada made cricket history by participating in the first country-against-country match in New York! Canada won by 23 runs after two days of play. Australia and England would go on to play each other and form the famous 'Ashes' competition, which is still played today. The British Empire was still very active in this part of history, so the practice of cricket spread far and wide and was embraced by most of the Commonwealth countries.

HOW HAS THE GAME EVOLVED OVER TIME?

Cricket has had a very interesting journey to its current standing and multiple variations. Given that the game originated as a pastime for children, it can be played by pretty much anyone. Over time, when specific teams and players gained fame for being particularly good at cricket, skills began to become a part of the game. While others had tried, Brian Lara, a famous cricketer from Trinidad and Tobago, masterminded pinpoint accurate batting. Shane Warne and Muttiah Muralitharan were two of the first players to consistently use the 'spin bowling technique', which added more skill and intricacy to that element of cricket. The very early versions of the game were played in open fields, but this changed with the introduction of cricket clubs, when they made pre-set play areas within the grounds.

More recently, advances in technology have allowed the game to change and be scored more accurately. Video replays allow tight decisions to be reviewed by the referee and his team to ensure they make the right call. Ball tracking tech has also allowed computers to measure things like throw speed, direction, trajectory, and other details, which can be very interesting and can be used for analysis.

Some decisions are so close that the referee can't review them by themselves. These decisions are passed on to another team of video referees. They look at game footage and then communicate with the referee via a headset, who can then inform the players and audience of the result. Such instances include when a ball looks like it touched the bat, a player's leg or the wicket, but it's difficult to be sure. Some games now use LED lights on their wickets that flash or light up when a ball has touched them, making it easier to tell.

The International Cricket Council

Early competitions between English counties and national teams were generally organised and governed by the two teams themselves. Cricket did not have an overarching authority, which led to differing rules and standards. They realized there needed to be one authority that all cricketers could follow and abide by.

In 1907, when the national team of South Africa wanted to visit England, the president of South African Cricket, Abe Bailey, was confused as to why the nations (England, Australia and South Africa) didn't collaborate more and organise international tournaments. He suggested the formation of an 'Imperial Cricket Conference', (changed in 1989 to International Cricket Council) with the concept of Test matches between the three nations. While the English were keen, the Australians did not warm to the idea. The inaugural tournaments in both 1909 and 1912 were not considered successes, with poor weather conditions and many cricketers refusing to play.

No further meetings of the ICC took place until 1921, because the nations were unable to agree on rules, but in 1926, George Harris, known as Lord Harris, an administrator for the Marylebone Cricket Club (MCC) in London, took a representative squad to Trinidad, where the West Indies team performed admirably against the English. The Caribbean team expressed a desire to play more games against nations like England and the other Test-playing teams.

Lord Harris, along with delegates from other countries, agreed that membership in the ICC should comprise *"governing bodies of cricket in countries within the Empire to which cricket teams are sent, or which send teams to England."*

West Indies played its first Test match in 1928 with New Zealand and India following in the next few years. From this point, the ICC would hold and conduct meetings on an annual basis. Today, the ICC is responsible for the global game and governance of cricket, mostly on international matters and rulings. There are national bodies like the English Cricket Board and Cricket Australia that manage the domestic games.

RULES OF CRICKET

No Rules and Clarifying of Rules

The first games of cricket were likely played with little structure other than hitting the ball and running, because they were played by children who hadn't defined the rules. When adults began to play for their counties, there began a tradition of meeting up for the game and then simply deciding the rules on that day. This would include number of players, overs, innings, and the distances for the game.

In 1727, when players and cricket club officials wanted to clarify the rules, many teams wanted participants to sign and adhere to the Articles of Agreement, which enforced the rules of any cricket match well before it was played. The 1744 code was one of the first official documents that stipulated specific rules that determined the sizing of stumps, bats, balls, and how many overs and innings were allowed, among other key rules.

Today's Rules

In today's version of the game, there are a few rules we should review here. When each team has completed one turn at batting and fielding, that's called a set of 'innings'. Within the innings, there are 'overs'. When a bowler is throwing the ball to a batter, he must deliver six legal balls (not high or wide) to the batsman. Once he's done that six times, his turn is over, and he must swap with another player on his team.

The number of innings and overs varies in the different distinctions of cricket. Test cricket, my grandfather's favourite, has unlimited overs for two innings. Those games can last a whole week! Some people prefer One Day Cricket, where the teams have either 40 or 50 overs for one innings. I like T20 the most, where each team has 20 overs in one innings, which usually lasts for around three hours. Some competitions have custom rules with different numbers of innings and overs, but the game is played the same way.

MOST FAMOUS CRICKET COMPETITIONS

The Cricket World Cup

Every cricket player dreams of winning the ICC's Cricket World Cup, as it is regarded as the richest prize in the sport. The first tournament took place in 1975, when it was hosted by England. The final took place at Lord's, a famous cricket ground in London, where the West Indies beat Australia by 17 runs.

England won the 2019 World Cup by defeating New Zealand. It was a great moment. My family and I celebrated for a long time. That's the only time England has won the competition. Australia holds the record for most World Cup wins, having won it six times! The last time was in 2023.

The Ashes

England and Australia share a friendship and rivalry in cricket. The teams have both been playing the sport for a very long time. They started playing each other in the 1870s, and one match in 1882 saw the Australians record their first win on English soil. After the loss, one English newspaper printed that English cricket had died and that "the body will be cremated, and the ashes taken to Australia." Then, the England captain, Ivo Bligh, said he would reclaim 'The Ashes,' thus creating the name of the traditional meeting between the two nations. After one meeting when England won the tournament in Australia, a member of the English team burnt parts of the wicket and a ball used in the game, put the ashes in an urn and brought them back to Marylebone Cricket Club as a trophy.

These games tend to be very tough contests. 73 Ashes series have been played as of 2023. Australia has won 34 times, England 32, and seven have been a draw.

Where is Cricket Played Now?

Cricket is a truly global game in today's world. While nations like England, Australia and South Africa are associated with the infancy of cricket, it is now played by people all over the world. The West Indies, while not a country itself, is a subregion and a general cricket term to refer to teams representing a multitude of nations and areas within the Caribbean and places nearby.

India is now seen as the most enthusiastic cricket nation, with the country enjoying plenty of success and forming the popular

Indian Premier League T20 competition in 2008. This competition boasts a large television viewership from around the globe. Neighbouring Pakistan and nearby island nation Sri Lanka also have passionate fan bases for the sport, with very good national teams.

Despite that, none of those nations have deemed it to be their national sport. Many Caribbean nations, on the other hand, like Barbados, Bermuda, Grenada, Guyana, Jamaica and the Turks and Caicos Islands, *have* made it their national sport. This illustrates the rich passion for cricket among the people of these regions. This has even led to the development of the Caribbean Premier League, another T20 tournament to rival the IPL.

England might not have as big a fan base as it used to or when compared to these other countries, but cricket is still played actively. When there's no football on TV during the summer, many often watch cricket instead. In addition to the county competitions, there is now 'The Hundred' competition, which is the English version of the IPL, with its T20 rules. This tournament has both men's and women's games playing at the same time.

While the ICC started with only three member nations, today it has expanded to 108 member countries! The most recent member admissions are Cambodia, the Ivory Coast and Uzbekistan, three countries from vastly different parts of the world, which shows the ever-growing appeal of cricket.

CULTURAL CHANGES TO INCLUDE WOMEN AND GIRLS

Despite the original game being played by children of both genders, the game has long been seen as a sport just for men and boys. However, the first record of a women's cricket match was in 1745. Women's cricket started to become more popular in the 1800s, with cricket clubs for women becoming more common. In 1926, the Women's Cricket Association began to formalise women's cricket just like the men's game.

As a matter of fact, when we were in school, my sister Jessica came to the same cricket training as me every week. There are no differences in the rules of the game the girls and professional women play – except they use a slightly smaller ball – which some people think should be changed to the same ball that the men use.

England's women's national team have won the World Cup more times than the men: four times! Jessica's favourite player is Tammy Beaumont, who has been playing for England since 2009.

TACTICS

Tactics play a major role in cricket. While the very early days might have been hit and hope, no contemporary top cricket game is without tactics and strategy. Given there are three distinct types of play: batting, bowling and fielding, teams will often try to make the most out of each play by organising their players in a distinct order.

A batting team might have a very good batter and could want them to go toward the end of the innings so they can enter the game when the opposing bowlers and fielders are a little more tired. This way, the batter has more chance of scoring many runs. Of course, the opposition might know that and save their best bowler until the elite batter takes to the field.

Batters and bowlers can use either their right or left hand, which can make for tricky situations, as the ball could come in or be batted in a different direction. Teams can try to match up their players to get an advantage over their opponents. Bowlers have the luxury of starting the run, meaning they can set the tone. They can also throw an especially fast or slow ball in order to confuse the batter.

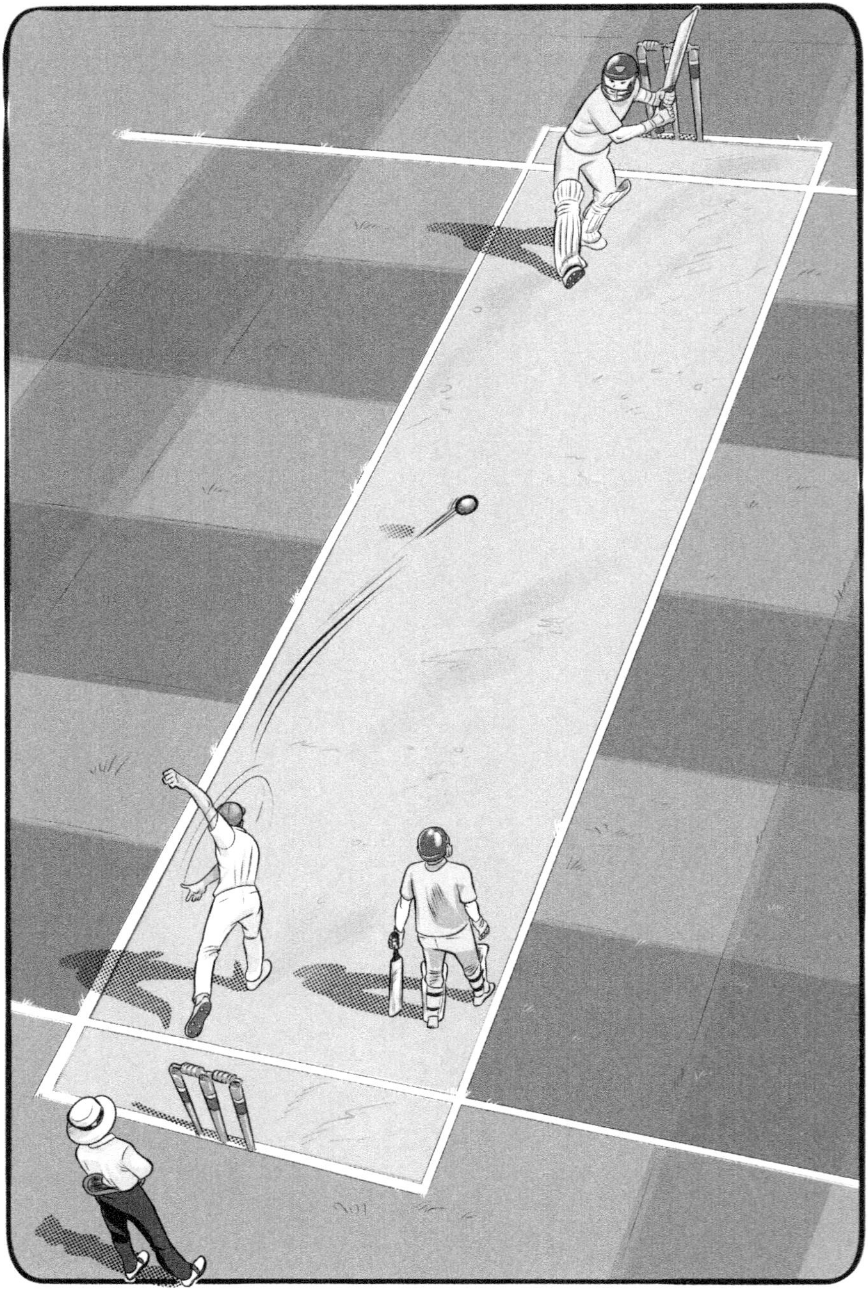

2

HOW CRICKET IS PLAYED

Okay, I know I briefly mentioned how cricket is played, but let's go through the rules in detail. Cricket is played between two teams of 11 players and one substitute, in case of injury. These teams take turns to bat and field. Let's go through the basics and what each team needs to do when they are batting or fielding.

CRICKET SETUP

Cricket is played on a round grass field. There are two sets of wooden stumps. One is the wicket, and the other is the bowling crease. The batter stands in front of the wicket, with the wicket-keeper from the other team standing behind it. The play area is also circular, and there is a small border around the zone. The wicket is made up of three wooden sticks stuck into the ground, with two smaller sticks, called bails, resting on top of those three.

The batter stands just ahead of the wicket within two white lines; this is where they can expect the ball to arrive when it is thrown toward them. The bowler throws the ball at the batter from the bowling crease. Most bowlers take a run-up to get more speed on their throw. The other players on the bowler's team are fielding and are called fielders, and the whole team is on the field at the same time. The other nine players on the batting team sit on the side-lines awaiting their turn.

BATTING TEAM

Two players from the batting team take to the field at the start of the game. One takes the position in front of the wicket and the other near the bowling crease. Batters must play in a pair and never be alone. When the bowler throws the ball toward them, the batter in front of the wicket will attempt to hit the ball with their bat. If the ball is hit, the two batting players can attempt to score runs.

To score a single run, the batting player must successfully swap places with their batting partner. If they make it to the other side without being knocked out of the game (we will look at this later), they earn one run for the team. But batters can score runs without even running. If a batter hits the border of the play area with the ball, this is called a **boundary**. By hitting the border of the field, the batter automatically scores four runs. Batters can score even more, though, by hitting the cricket ball over boundaries. This is called a **maximum** and scores six runs!

The batting team continues trying to score runs until ten batters have been knocked out by the fielding team or if the bowlers run out of overs. After this, the teams change over so the batting team is now fielding, and the field team is now batting.

FIELDING TEAM

The fielding team will try to stop the batting team from scoring runs by trying to eliminate the batting team's players using a variety of methods. When the bowler aims the ball, they are trying to hit the wicket. If the batter doesn't hit the ball and the ball hits the wicket and knocks over the bails, the batter is **bowled out** and must go to the side-lines, as they are out of the game.

If the batter hits the ball into the air, but the fielder immediately catches it (without it bouncing on the ground), they will be **caught out**. A batter might hit the ball and then start to run for their partner's crease; even if the fielders don't catch it immediately, they can still throw it at the wicket – if this is done before the batter returns to the crease or wicket, then they will be **run out**. This can happen when a batter tries to score multiple runs.

Another way that the fielding team can knock out batters is by **LBW**. This is where a bowled ball hits a batter's leg. Usually, when this happens, one of the referees or umpires will review the throw (with replay technology) and will decide if the original throw would have hit the wicket if the batter's leg hadn't been in the way. If it was going to hit the wicket, the batter is out; if not, they bowl again. Sometimes, the batter might miss the ball, but the ball won't hit the wicket. This is when the wicketkeeper comes in. The wicketkeeper can catch the ball from behind the wicket and throw it at the bails. The batter will then be **stumped out**.

There are a few other ways batters can be knocked out that aren't so common:

· Accidentally hitting their wicket

· If they hit the ball twice in one play

- If they handle the ball – accidentally or on purpose

- Obstructing a fielding player

- Taking too long to enter the field of play

These five ways are very rare, though, so don't expect to see them the next time you watch cricket.

What Are Overs?

When a bowler is throwing a ball to the batter, they must throw 'six legal balls'. This means the ball is not high or wide of the white markings that the batter is standing within. When six legal balls have been thrown, that is known as an **over**. Games set numbers of overs; this means that both teams have a fair chance to score the same number of runs. Different variations of cricket have varying amounts of overs.

HOW THE GAME PLAYS OUT

During the game, batters will try to score runs while the fielders will try to stop them by taking them out of the game using one of the methods listed above. The batters will continue their turn until one of two things happens: 1) if 10 of the 11 players are eliminated, as the last batter is not allowed to stay on the field by himself, or 2) if they 'run out of overs'.

Then, the teams swap places and do it all over again with the roles reversed. The batters now must field and bowl. This means, of course, that cricket players need to be good at every part of the game and not just rely on one particular skill. When both teams have had a chance to bat and field, that is the conclusion of the **innings**. This is the cricket word for round. If a game has multiple innings, it means that all the players who were knocked out of the first innings can now return to play for the second. Some games have multiple innings, which can take a very long time to play, sometimes even a week or more!

THE WEATHER

Sometimes the weather can play a big role in how cricket is played. The ideal setting is bright, clear sunshine. In very hot countries, sometimes the players have to wear special white paint to cover parts of their face and body so they don't get sunburned. If it rains, the game cannot be played, which can lead to matches being suspended, interrupted or even cancelled. This is usually called being rained off.

In longer games, where one team has significantly less time to bat because of rain, officials use the Duckworth-Lewis method. This takes into account how much realistic game time they have left and changes the target they have to meet to defeat their opponents, who concluded their innings without a rain delay. If the rain impacts the start of play and neither team has completed their innings, the officials may decide to reduce each team's overs. One stadium in the world, the Docklands Stadium in Melbourne, Australia, has a retractable roof, which means if it rains, the game can continue under the roof.

Other issues, like poor visibility, wind and heat can also play a major role in how the game is played, with teams having to change their strategy due to the changing conditions. There is a way for cricket matches to avoid all these adverse weather conditions, though: Play inside! Indoor cricket, however, is not common and not very popular.

CRICKET VARIATIONS

As I mentioned earlier, there are a few different variations of cricket. The main three are Test Cricket, One Day International and T20. Let's look at what differentiates them from one another.

Test Cricket

Test cricket is the oldest style of cricket. Some people like this variation because there are no limits for overs, as all the batters must be dismissed or retire to end the innings. These games are usually played over two innings, so can take quite a while, with some lasting for days. Given that play can start early in the morning and go until the evening, it is not uncommon for the players to break for lunch. How many other sports do that? The look of Test cricket is still very traditional, as the players often wear all-white uniforms, which are made out of wool or other soft fabrics.

One Day International Cricket

One Day International Cricket, as the name suggests, is a competition that typically starts and finishes within a single day. The teams are usually limited to either 40 or 50 overs (depending on the classification of the match and playing conditions). ODI is often seen as a variation of Test cricket and T20. While counties and cricket clubs play Test cricket and T20, it is not common for any team other than an international team to play ODI or ODI rules. The uniforms that these players wear tend to be more colourful than the Test cricket players and usually have the name of the country across the middle of the shirt.

T20 Cricket and Other Short-form Variations

Some think that the other types of cricket are too long. T20 cricket was made to make the sport more exciting and fast-paced. The name T20 is a shortening of 'Twenty20', and refers to the maximum number of overs allowed, as each team is allowed to bowl and receive only 20 overs. These games typically last around three hours. The first T20 competition was held in 2003 between English counties, and the Surrey Lions won the first tournament. The first international T20 game was held in 2004 between the women's teams of England and New Zealand. The New Zealand team won this match by nine runs.

Some people say that the rules and general look of T20 makes it the most modern version of cricket. The teams often wear brightly coloured uniforms, which are made out of the same material as football shirts. T20 generally has lots of advertising, so teams can have sponsors, and even the wickets can have a company logo on them!

Some versions are very similar to T20. One is called T10, and as you've probably guessed, the teams only have ten overs each. This variation is popular and commonly played in the UAE, Zimbabwe and by the European Cricket League. The Hundred is a new form of cricket based on T20. Instead of limiting the number of overs, it stipulates a set number of balls, meaning that overs aren't counted.

3

THE BEST CRICKET PLAYERS

In this chapter, we'll learn about some of the best cricket players from past and present. All these people are accomplished in their own right and contributed to many successes for their respective teams. These are some of my favourites. Sometimes, my father and grandfather argue about who is better among some of the older players, but the truth is, all of them are exceptional players.

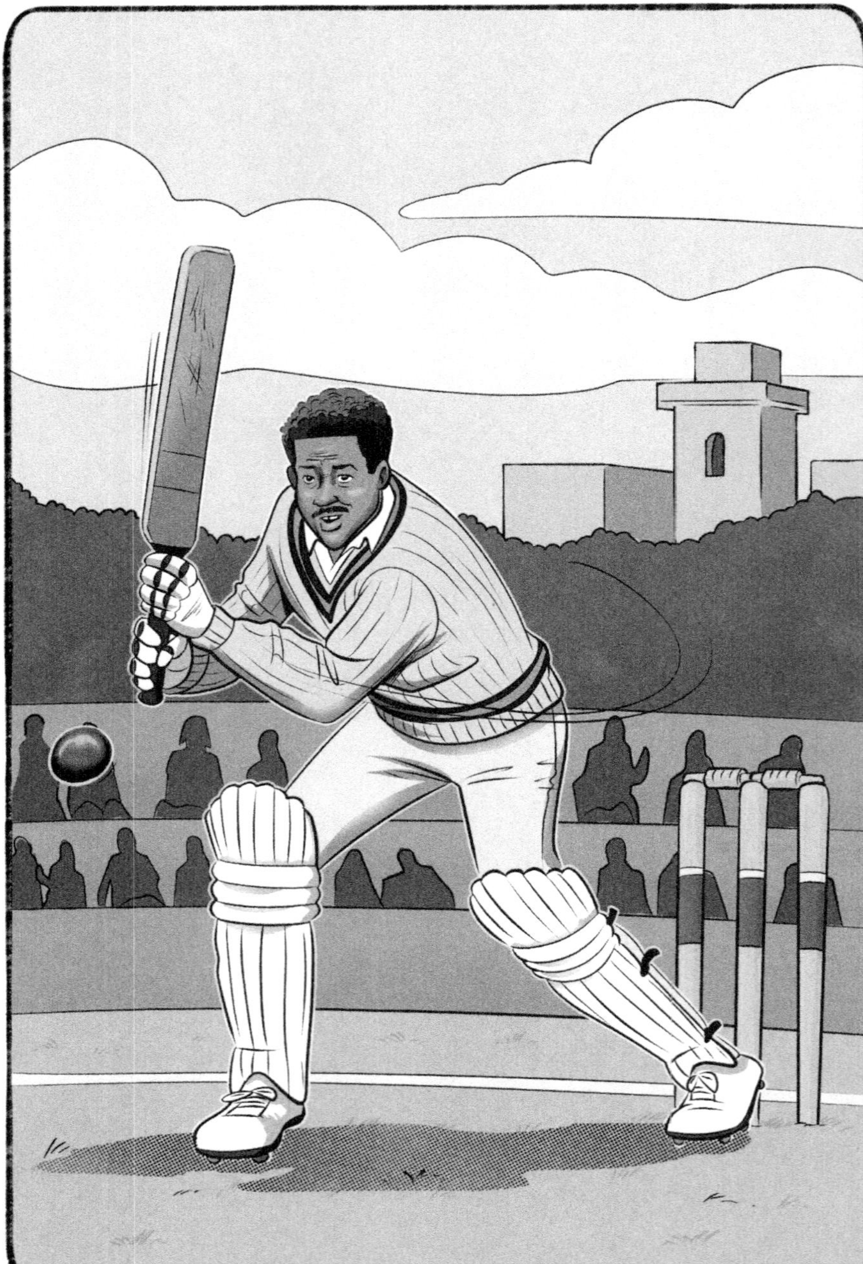

GARFIELD SOBERS

Full Name: Sir Garfield St Aubrun Sobers

Born: 28th July, 1936

Hometown: Bridgetown, Barbados

Nationality: Barbadian

Role: All-rounder

Teams: West Indies, Barbados, South Australia, Nottinghamshire

Regarded as one of the best cricket players of all time, Garfield Sobers scored over 8,000 runs and took more than 200 wickets, which was quite an accomplishment, given that cricket was played a lot less during this time. The Barbadian played for the West Indies international team for 20 years and served as the captain for half of his career.

Despite being revered as a West Indies legend, Sobers had retired from international cricket by the time the team won the Cricket World Cup in 1975. One of his few international awards came from the Shell Shield the year before, when he represented Barbados, which left his nation on an undefeated campaign. He was also named the Wisden Cricketer of the Century in 2000.

One of his most memorable performances saw him notch up 365 runs (that's one for each day of the year!) against Pakistan in 1957. This was part of a Test series in Kingston, Jamaica. He showed exceptional longevity at the highest level of cricket as he put in another vintage performance in 1966, when he took six wickets against England, allowing them just 73 runs. He would then go on to score 174 runs by himself.

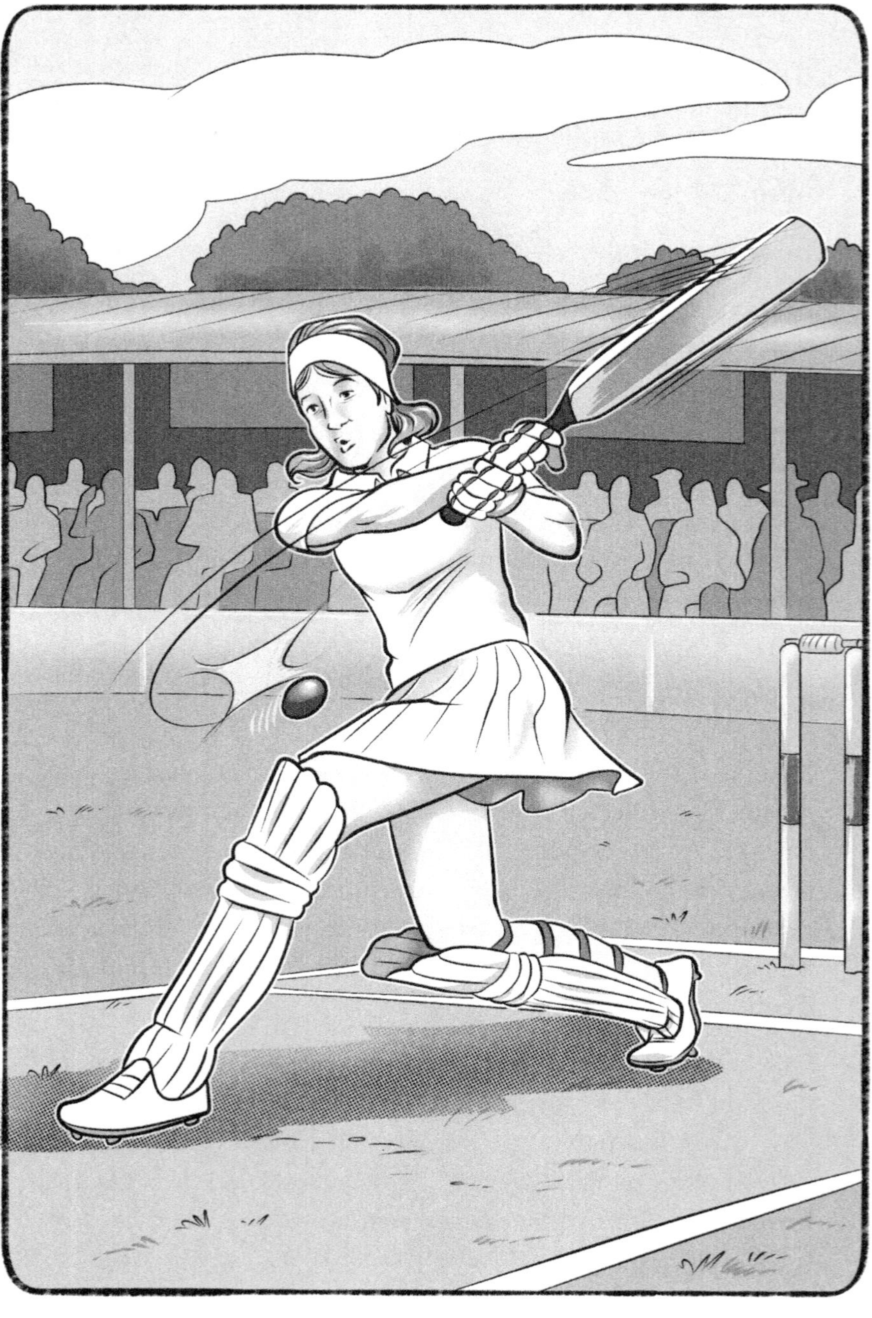

RACHAEL HEYHOE FLINT

Full Name: Rachael Heyhoe Flint

Born: 11th June, 1939

Hometown: Wolverhampton, England

Nationality: English

Died: 18th January, 2017

Role: Batter

Teams: England, West Midlands, West of England, East Midlands, Warwickshire

Rachael Heyhoe Flint might be one of the most influential women in cricket to have ever stepped on the field. She first appeared in the England national team back in 1960, and after six years, she was promoted to full-time captain. She led the team for 12 years, and during her tenure, the England team didn't lose a single match! Flint was instrumental in the English team winning the first-ever Women's Cricket World Cup in 1973, as she scored a century (100 or more runs in a single innings) in the tournament. Flint wasn't just a talented cricketer; she played hockey at a professional level and took up a career in politics later in life.

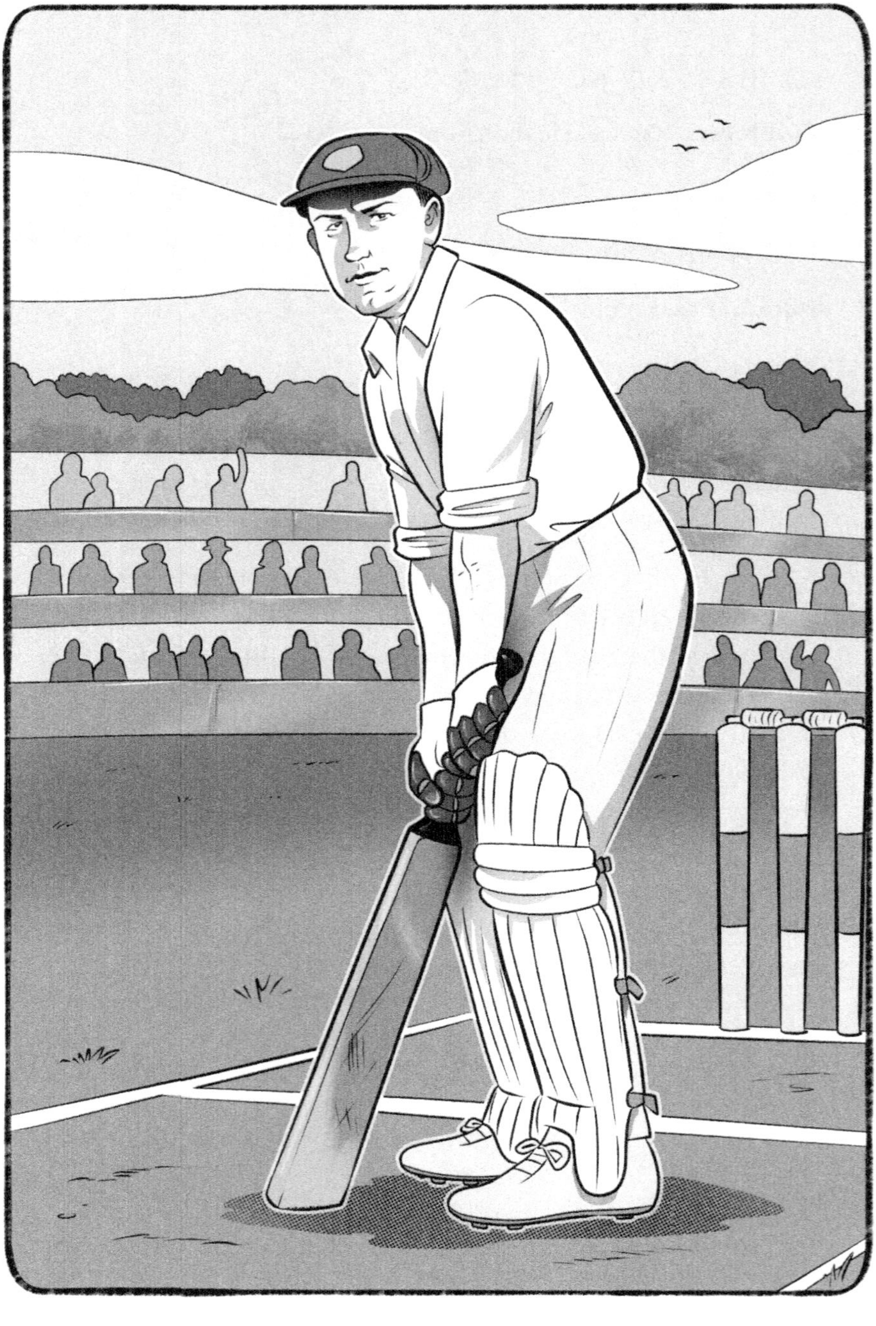

DON BRADMAN

Full Name: Sir Donald George Bradman

Nickname: The Don

Born: 27th August, 1908

Hometown: New South Wales, Australia

Nationality: Australian

Died: 25th February 2001

Role: Batsman

Teams: Australia, New South Wales, South Australia

Affectionately known as 'The Don', Donald Bradman is regarded as one of the greatest batsmen of all time. Bradman very rarely had a bad game, as he averaged 99 runs per Test match, making him incredibly prolific and leading Australia to think they could win any game when he was in the squad.

The iconic batsman led Australia to glory in multiple Test fixtures against many of the nations they played. Given his ability to score, he was labelled as a national hero and considered Australia's first international celebrity. Bradman loved to play against England, especially at Headingley Stadium in Leeds. In 1930, he scored 334 runs and then, three years later, another 304!

NAT SCIVER-BRUNT

Full Name: Natalie Ruth Sciver-Brunt

Born: 20th August, 1992

Born in: Tokyo, Japan

Nationality: English

Role: All-rounder

Teams: England, Surrey, Melbourne Stars, Surrey Stars, Perth Scorchers, Supernovas, Northern Diamonds, Trent Rockets, Mumbai Indians, The Blaze.

Despite being born in Tokyo, Japan, Nat Sciver-Brunt is very much an Englishwoman, with hundreds of appearances for the England national team. She's shown on multiple occasions that she has an eye for runs, with eight centuries in One Day International matches, four of them against Australia. She was at the heart of the 2017 Cricket World Cup final win for England, as she scored 51 runs against India to claim the trophy at Lord's in London.

Sciver-Brunt made history by being part of the Mumbai Indians team that won the first-ever Women's Premier League competition. She scored 332 runs in the tournament – the second-highest of all players. This included 60 in the final match, where the game ended before she was dismissed.

PAUL COLLINGWOOD

Full Name: Paul David Collingwood

Nickname: Colly

Born: 26th May, 1976

Hometown: County Durham, England

Nationality: English

Role: All-rounder

Teams: England, Durham, Delhi Daredevils, Rajasthan Royals, Perth Scorchers, Impi.

There were many English heroes from 2005 when England won the Ashes, breaking a nearly 20-year cycle of Australian dominance in the series. Paul Collingwood, however, typified this era for English cricket with great success as he scored over 1,000 runs in 2006 and a double century against Australia the following year. Another key game for Collingwood was the One Day International against Bangladesh in 2005, where he scored 112 runs. Collingwood would serve as the captain in the 2010 T20 World Cup, when England won the entire tournament, again beating Australia in the final.

Collingwood was also incredibly proficient at catching the ball and, at one point, held the record for the most catches by an England player who wasn't a wicketkeeper. His varied skill set and longevity led him to a 10-year career with the national team.

SHAHEEN AFRIDI

Full Name: Shaheen Shah Afridi

Nickname: The Eagle

Born: 6th April, 2000

Hometown: Khyber Pakhtunkhwa, Pakistan

Nationality: Pakistani

Role: Bowler

Teams: Pakistan, Khan Research, Lahore Qalanders, Balochistan, Northern, Hampshire, Khyber Pakhtunkhwa, Middlesex, Nottinghamshire, Welsh Fire, Dhaka Dynamites, Rotterdam Rhinos, Team White, Team Green, Birmingham Phoenix, Comilla Victorians.

The ICC elected Shaheen Afridi as the Player of the Year in 2021, as he took 78 wickets in just 36 international matches during the year. Afridi was named the T20 international captain after excelling in this discipline, helping Pakistan reach the final of the 2022 World Cup. He has continued to enjoy a good career in the English county system, having helped Nottinghamshire rebuild itself as a Division One team at the tender age of 23.

Potentially his best performance came in the 2018 Asia Cup when he secured five wickets, limiting Afghanistan to 35 runs during that over. The Eagle has, on rare occasions, shown abilities with the bat, having been named the Player of the Match in a One Day International game against Zimbabwe in 2020. In this particular fixture, he was able to take five wickets for 49 runs and scored 21 himself when the teams changed around.

ASHLEIGH GARDENER

Full Name: Ashleigh Katherine Gardner

Born: 15th April, 1997

Hometown: New South Wales, Australia

Nationality: Australian

Role: All-rounder

Teams: Australia, New South Wales, Sydney Sixers, Northern Districts, South Australia, Gujarat Giants.

The Belinda Clark Award is seen by many as the highest honour that an Australian female cricketer can receive because it's considered recognition of exceptional play. Ashleigh Gardener was bestowed this award in 2022. The three-time T20 champion added both the Women's World Cup and a gold medal from the 2022 Commonwealth Games to her trophy cabinet.

Gardner famously scored a century of runs against England within her first year of playing with the national team in 2017. Three years later, she put in another shift against the same opposition in the 2020 T20 World Cup final. Australia batted first when she scored a handsome 78 runs. After that, she took two wickets for 34 runs, which was a major factor in Australia winning both the game and the championship.

SOPHIE ECCLESTONE

Full Name: Sophie Ecclestone

Born: 6th May, 1999

Hometown: Chester, England

Nationality: England

Role: Bowler

Teams: Cheshire, Lancashire, Lancashire Thunder, Trailblazers, North West Thunder, Manchester Originals, Supernovas, Sydney Sixers, UP Warriorz

If you need a wicket, you can rely on Sophie Ecclestone. While growing up, there weren't many opportunities for girls to play cricket in her area, so she played with the boys and regularly upset them when she bowled them out. Ecclestone took that proficiency well beyond the schoolyard as she became the youngest woman to take 50 wickets in WT20I cricket in just 34 matches. This led to her being named the best bowler in T20 cricket in 2020.

The bowler has shown the capacity to perform in the biggest cricket games, performing her best in matches against top-class opponents like India and Australia. In 2018, when playing India, she took four wickets, limiting the Indian batters to just 18 runs. A year later, also in T20I, she took three wickets for 22 runs against the Australian team.

Ecclestone has had a decorated career already but has also finished as a runner-up many times. She's reached many finals with England and even played with the Sydney Sixers in the Big Bash. While the team topped the regular season standings, they lost out in the championship final.

SURYAKUMAR YADAV

Full Name: Suryakumar Yadav

Nickname: SKY

Born: 14th September, 1990

Hometown: Bombay, India

Nationality: Indian

Role: Batter

Teams: India, Parsi Gymkhana Club, Mumbai, Mumbai Indians, Kolkata Knight Riders.

It took Suryakumar Yadav a long time to break into the Indian national team, but he's now one of the regular team members. He played active parts in the Indian team that won the ACC Asia Cup in 2023, as well as in India's journey to the Cricket World Cup final in the same year. Before those achievements, Yadav enjoyed lots of success in T20, winning the Indian Premier League four times during his time with the Mumbai Indians and the Kolkata Knight Riders.

One of his most impressive performances came in the 2020 IPL season while playing for the Mumbai Indians. In the game against the Royal Challengers Bangalore, he scored 79 runs from just 43 balls. This result was the difference between his team finishing at the top of the IPL table and finishing third that season. The Mumbai Indians would go on to win the entire competition for 2020.

ROHIT SHARMA

Full Name: Rohit Gurunath Sharma

Nickname: Hitman

Born: 30th April, 1987

Hometown: Nagpur, India

Nationality: Indian

Role: Batter

Teams: India, Mumbai, Deccan Chargers, Mumbai Indians

India has been at the top of the cricket world for many years now. That seems to run alongside having the excellent Rohit Sharma. He is now the Indian national team captain and has helped his country win the T20 World Cup, win many Asian trophies and reach the ICC Cricket World Cup final in 2023. He has regularly been praised by the ICC, was named the ODI cricketer of the year in 2019, and has received many other similar awards.

Sharma was a formidable player in the 2010s. In 2014, in a One Day International match against Sri Lanka, he scored 264 runs, which at the time was the highest score by an individual in ODI cricket. The next year he hit a lightning-quick T20 century after just 62 balls against South Africa. He would also score five centuries throughout the 2019 World Cup, as India made it to the semi-final.

Winning the IPL six times, Sharma is considered a national hero in India, both with the Mumbai Indians and his former team, the Deccan Chargers. His captaincy with the Mumbai Indians has been credited as the reason the franchise has been one of the most successful in the competition. In 2015, he received the Arjuna Award from his country's government for his sporting excellence. Five years later, he was awarded the highest sporting honour in India with the Major Dhyan Chand Khel Ratna Award.

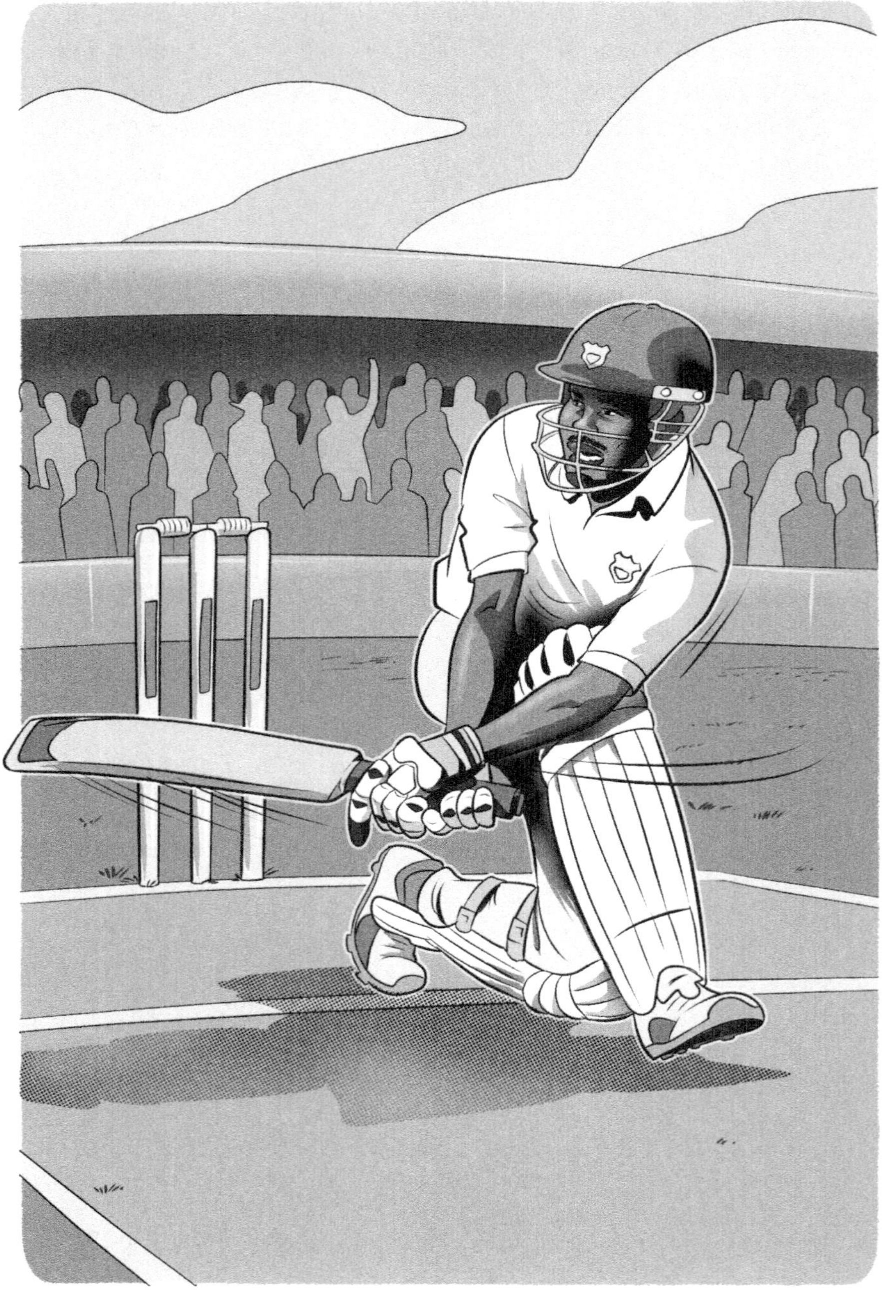

BRIAN LARA

Full Name: Brian Charles Lara

Born: 2nd May, 1969

Hometown: Santa Cruz, Trinidad and Tobago

Nationality: Trinidadian

Role: Batsman

Former Teams: West Indies, Trinidad and Tobago, Northern Transvaal, Warwickshire, Southern Rocks.

One of the greatest batsmen of all time, Brian Lara was a gifted run-scorer in cricket. He amassed over 11,000 runs in just 131 Test matches, making him one of the most efficient batters to have ever played the game.

Lara loved playing against England. Ten years before his famous 400 score, he scored 375 runs against the same opposition. Yet, he was a hero to some English cricket fans, as he played exceptionally well for Warwickshire. In 1994, he scored 2,006 runs for the county team as they lifted the County Championship. This included a 501 not-out performance against Durham.

Lara's time for the West Indies was unfortunately not the most successful for the team, as they recorded very few tournament wins despite the participation of the legendary batsman. Lara did, however, serve as the captain during the 2004 ICC Champions Trophy, in which the team defeated England in the final at the Oval in London. Three years later, with the West Indies hosting the 2007 Cricket World Cup, Lara was given a standing ovation as he played his last international match.

SMRITI MANDHANA

Full Name: Smriti Shriniwas Mandhana

Born: 18th July, 1996

Hometown: Mumbai, India

Nationality: Indian

Role: Batter

Teams: India, Maharashtra, Brisbane Heat, Hobart Hurricanes, Western Storm, Trailblazers, Southern Brave, Sydney Thunder, Royal Challengers Bangalore.

There are few more prolific figures in women's cricket than Smriti Mandhana. She is often used as an opening batter, given her ability to start matches with decent scoring records, having commonly scored an average of 20-45 runs in every discipline of cricket. As a teenager, she was part of the team that won the 2016 T20 World Cup and has continually turned out for India, winning Asian titles and reaching many international finals.

Mandhana rose to international prominence at the T20 World Cup in the West Indies, where she was comfortably one of the best batters as India reached the semi-finals. She scored an impressive 72 runs in the opening game against New Zealand and 83 against the eventual champions Australia in the final group-stage match.

In addition to her successes with India, Mandhana has also played well for domestic teams, winning The Hundred competition in 2023 with Southern Brave, and putting in some great performances against the Trent Rockets and the Welsh Fire.

JOE ROOT

Full Name: Joe Edward Root

Born: 30th December, 1990

Hometown: Sheffield, England

Nationality: English

Role: Batsman

Teams: England, Yorkshire, Sydney Thunder, Trent Rockets. Dubai Capitals, Rajasthan Royals.

The top-order batsman, Joe Root, has been an integral part of the England team since joining the national setup in 2012. While his awards and triumphs are rich and vast, he became the leading run-scorer in the 2019 World Cup when England won the tournament. Another key milestone that Root secured was scoring 10,000 runs in Test cricket, becoming just the second Englishman to do so.

Despite being a proud Yorkshireman, one of Root's finest performances came in Lancashire at Old Trafford Cricket Ground. In a 2016 Test match against Pakistan, he scored an excellent double-century with 254 runs, one of the highest individual scores in Test cricket history. He would also find success at the same venue four years later as he recorded another high score of 184 against the West Indies.

Root has also scored 46 international centuries, making him one of the most prolific run-scorers in cricket history. However, he's also enjoyed success with Yorkshire, winning two County Championships and the 2022 Hundred title with the Trent Rockets.

KAGISO RABADA

Full Name: Kagiso Rabada

Nickname: KG

Born: 25th May, 1995

Hometown: Johannesburg, South Africa

Nationality: South African

Role: Bowler

Teams: South Africa, Gauteng, DP World Lions, Kent, Delhi Capitals, Jozi Stars, Punjab Kings.

Since Kagiso Rabada's emergence in the South African national team, the country has had no problem taking wickets and dismissing opposition players. In July 2018, he became the youngest player to reach 150 wickets in Test cricket, at 23 years old.

While Rabada hasn't won any silverware with South Africa just yet, he has won both Test and T20 competitions with the DP World Lions. In addition, he was part of the Jozi Stars team that won the first-ever Mzansi Super League competition. He also played a massive role in Kent securing promotion back to the first division of the County Championship in 2016.

2018 might have been Rabada's favourite year to date. He was named the ICC Cricketer of the Year, not only for reaching the 150 wicket mark but also for taking six wickets for 54 runs against Australia in a Test match, becoming the 'Man of the Series', as well.

MARIZANNE KAPP

Full Name: Marizanne Kapp

Nickname: Kappie

Born: 4th January, 1990

Hometown: Port Elizabeth, South Africa

Nationality: South African

Role: All-rounder

Former Teams: South Africa, Eastern Province, Northerns, Sydney Sixers, Surrey, Surrey Stars, Australian, Capital Territory, Oval Invincibles, Perth Scorchers, Delhi Capitals, Barbados Royals, Sydney Thunder.

Marizanne Kapp might be the most well-rounded cricketer in South African history. She's been part of the South Africa team since 2009. One of her formative performances came back in a T20I match in 2010 against New Zealand. First, she took four wickets for 29 runs before going on to score 34 of her runs with the bat.

She has since played a prominent part in their semi-final appearances in the Cricket World Cup in both 2017 and 2022. In addition to being a prolific scorer in Test cricket, she bowled nine wickets in the 2023 T20 World Cup when South Africa made it to the final on home soil.

Kappie has ingrained herself into women's cricket history, as she was part of the Barbados Royals team that won the Women's Caribbean Premier League in 2023. She has also played a very active role for the Oval Invincibles in England,

and was named the Player of the Match in the 2022 final when her team won the championship.

BABAR AZAM

Full Name: Babar Azam

Nickname: Bobby

Born: 15th October, 1994

Hometown: Lahore, Pakistan

Nationality: Pakistani

Role: Batter

Teams: Pakistan, Zarai Taraqiati Bank, Islamabad Leopards, State Bank of Pakistan, Sui Southern Gas Corporation, Islamabad United, Karachi Kings, Guyana Amazon Warriors, Sylhet Sixers, Somerset, Central Punjab, Peshawar Zalmi.

One of the best batters in cricket right now is Babar Azam. In 2021, after securing his 13th ODI century, he was named the top ODI batsman, surpassing the previous record of 865 points. This led to being named the ICC's cricketer of the year. 2021 provided many milestones for Babar as he also earned his 8,000th run in international cricket! Unfortunately for Azam, his Pakistani national team isn't at the same level as him. He resigned from his responsibilities as captain across all three disciplines after Pakistan's disappointing outing at the 2023 World Cup.

Before that, however, Azam was incredibly prolific for Pakistan in the late 2010s. In just his third One Day International match, he scored 125 against West Indies. Since then, he has gone on to specialise in ODI format cricket, notably notching up another 115 against Sri Lanka in 2017.

While his national team hasn't always won competitions, Azam has made up for it with heroic performances in domestic tournaments, dedicating most of his career to the Pakistani Super League. He's won that competition with Islamabad United and the Karachi Kings.

HAYLEY MATTHEWS

Full Name: Hayley Kristen Matthews

Born: 19th March, 1998

Hometown: Bridgetown, Barbados

Nationality: Barbadian

Role: All-rounder

Teams: West Indies, Barbados, Tasmania, Hobart Hurricanes, Lancashire Thunder, Southern Vipers, Velocity, Loughborough Lightning, Welsh Fire, Trailblazers, Barbados Royals, Melbourne Renegades, Mumbai Indians.

Current West Indies captain Hayley Matthews excels in both batting and bowling for the national team. Matthews has scored six centuries across both One Day Internationals and T20 cricket, and was named the player of the final in the 2016 T20 World Cup final when the West Indies defeated Australia at Eden Gardens in Kolkata, India. This came as she scored 100 runs not out, which allowed the West Indies to win the tournament. 2016 was a fine year for Matthews, as she also made a century score of 117 against South Africa in One Day International cricket.

She was also part of the first-ever Women's Premier League championship-winning side in India, scoring 271 runs and taking 16 wickets for the Mumbai Indians. Those wickets were enough for her to be awarded the purple cap, the prize for the best bowler in the tournament. Matthews became captain of the Barbados Royals team in the Caribbean Premier League in 2023.

JASPRIT BUMRAH

Full Name: Jasprit Jasbirsingh Bumrah

Born: 6th December, 1993

Hometown: Gujarat, India

Nationality: Indian

Role: Bowler

Teams: India, Gujarat, Mumbai Indians

Jasprit Bumrah gained instant fame when he first started playing in the Indian Premier League, when he put in classic performances for the Mumbai Indians. Unlike many cricketers, Bumrah has stayed with one franchise throughout his career and only ever played for this team in T20 cricket. Here he has won the IPL championship five times! At the end of the 2023 season, he had 130 wickets for the team, which is only 40 off the all-time team record.

He has also played a lot for the Indian national team, taking hundreds of wickets for the country. His skills have helped India win multiple championships in Asia, most recently taking home the ACC Asia Cup in 2023 and reaching the final of the World Cup in the same year. Bumrah also had an exceptional end to the 2010 decade. In a 2019 Test match against the West Indies, he bowled five wickets for only seven runs, silencing the crowd in Antigua. In the same year, he took 18 wickets in just nine innings in the 2019 Cricket World Cup.

CHAMARI ATHAPATHTHU

Full Name: Atapattu Mudiyanselage Chamari Jayangani

Born: 9th February, 1990

Hometown: Kurunegala, Sri Lanka

Nationality: Sri Lankan

Role: Batter

Teams: Sri Lanka, Yorkshire Diamonds, Melbourne Renegades, Loughborough Lightning, Supernovas, Perth Scorchers, Sydney Thunder.

Very few athletes have a dedicated seating area in a stadium for supporters when they are still active in their careers. But Chamari Athapaththu, who plays with the Sydney Thunder, because of her popularity, will have a special area named after her, Chamari Bay, at the Sydney Cricket Ground. She previously played with the Melbourne Renegades and even won the Women's Big Bash League during her short stay with the Perth Scorchers.

While she has enjoyed playing franchise cricket, she has also had a stellar career with Sri Lanka, including eight century scores, with one coming against Australia, where she scored 178 and wasn't dismissed. She was part of the silver medal-winning team at the Asian Games in China in 2022. Athapaththu recorded one of the highest-ever scores in women's One Day International cricket in 2017, scoring 178 runs against Australia in the World Cup that year. She loves to play against the Australians, scoring 113 against them in T20 and another 153 in Test cricket.

SHAKIB AL HASAN

Full Name: Khondaker Sakib Al-Hassan

Nickname: Faysal

Born: 24th March, 1987

Hometown: Magura, Bangladesh

Nationality: Bangladeshi

Role: All-rounder

Teams: Bangladesh, Khulna Division, Worchestershire, Kolkata Knight Riders, Barbados Tridents, Jamaica Tallawahs, Dhaka Dominators, Karachi Kings, Sunrisers Hyderabad, Guyana Amazon Warriors, Fortune Barishal, Peshawar Zalmi, Galle Titans, Montreal Tigers.

While Bangladesh might not have the same cricketing ability as nearby countries like India and Pakistan, the country boasts a player that gives them a chance to defeat higher-ranked opponents. Shakib Al Hasan scores runs and takes wickets for Bangladesh, and has been a major part of the national team since 2006.

Within just a few years of being on the national team, Al Hasan was already making headlines in Bangladeshi cricket. One notable performance came in Chattogram, when he first scored a Test century while batting and then took five wickets for just 47 runs against New Zealand in 2008. The following year, he scored 144 runs before taking six wickets against Pakistan, allowing them only 82 runs. His longevity has served both him and his country well. He was one of the best players at the 2019 World Cup, where he scored 606 runs despite Bangladesh finishing eighth overall.

Al Hasan is potentially one of the most well-travelled cricketers. He's won the Pakistani League with Peshawar Zalmi, the Bangladesh Premier League during his time with the Dhaka Dominators and even lifted the Caribbean Premier League with two different teams. In 2023, he won the Global T20 Canada competition in his first season with the Montreal Tigers.

LAURA WOLVAARDT

Full Name: Laura Wolvaardt

Born: 26th April, 1999

Hometown: Western Cape, South Africa

Nationality: South African

Role: Batter

Teams: South Africa, Western Province, Brisbane Heat, Adelaide Strikers, Northern Superchargers, Velocity, Gujarat Giants, Manchester Originals, Northerns.

Laura Wolvaardt has expertly showcased the technical ability to read bowler's balls and make the right shot selection almost every time she takes to the field to bat. She has batted an average of 45 runs in her One Day International career for South Africa.

In 2016, Wolvaardt was virtually unstoppable in ODI cricket as she tore up Ireland in a series of matches. In just her second One Day International match, she made a century score of 105 and became the youngest South African woman to score over 100 runs in a single game. She continued her rich form in the same series when she later scored 149 runs against the Irish. Her efforts have made South Africa one of the better teams in women's cricket as they have progressed deeper in big tournaments and famously made the final in the T20 World Cup in 2023.

As well as playing very well for South Africa, Wolvaardt has made a name for herself in Australia, winning the Women's Big Bash League twice with the Adelaide Strikers. She famously scored 403 runs in the 2022-23 season, when her team won the overall tournament. She was also part of the 2018-19 Brisbane Heat team that won the competition at the Gabba.

RASHID KHAN

Full Name: Rashid Khan Arman

Born: 20th September, 1998

Hometown: Nangarhar Province, Afghanistan

Nationality: Afghanistan

Role: All-rounder

Teams: Afghanistan, Comilla Victorians, Sunrisers Hyderabad, Guyana Amazon Warriors, Band-e-Amir Dragons, Adelaide Strikers, Sussex, Kabul Zwanan, Durban Heat, Barbados Tridents, Lahore Qalandars, Gujarat Titans, St Kitts & Nevis Patriots, MI Cape Town, MI New York.

While known as an all-round player, Rashid Khan possesses some of the best bowling skills to have ever been seen on a cricket turf. His spin bowling technique is just one of his exceptional delivery methods, which have ensured that Afghanistan takes many wickets. Khan has been prolific across all disciplines of cricket but statistically the best in Test, averaging 22 wickets per game.

He has also played in a wide variety of T20 franchise competitions with decent success. This includes winning the Shpageeza Cricket League in his native Afghanistan with Band-e-Amir Dragons and the Big Bash League with the Adelaide Strikers. He has played for the Australian team since 2017 and is now the leading bowler for Adelaide Strikers, with 98 wickets. Khan has a cult following from the Sunrisers Hyderabad supporters, because he took three wickets in the 2018 Indian Premier League final, which helped the team win the championship title against the Chennai Super Kings.

SOPHIE DEVINE

Full Name: Sophie Frances Monique Devine

Born: 1st September, 1989

Hometown: Porirua, New Zealand

Nationality: Kiwi (New Zealander)

Role: All-rounder

Teams: New Zealand, Wellington, Canterbury. South Australia, Adelaide Strikers, Loughborough Lightning, Warwickshire, Yorkshire Diamonds, Supernovas, Western Australia, Perth Scorchers, Birmingham Phoenix, Royal Challengers Bangalore, Guyana Amazon Warriors.

Sophie Devine is an exceptional all-round cricketer with skills across both batting and bowling. Coupled with her leadership qualities, Devine has become a central figure in the New Zealand national team, having served as captain for many years now. Despite her advancing years, she is still scoring centuries and has now made seven for New Zealand in her career. Such skills helped the Kiwis get to the T20 World Cup final in both 2009 and 2010. She has continued to be an aggressive batter who consistently scores runs, even at the tail end of her career. In 2017, she famously scored 93 runs from just 41 balls in an ODI match against Pakistan.

Despite representing New Zealand, Devine has plenty of history-making efforts and records from her career in the Australian Women's Big Bash League. She was able to lift a trophy in her domestic cricket career when she played with the WBBL-winning Perth Scorchers in the 2020-21 season. She has been prolific in Australian franchise cricket, scoring 769 runs in a single season when playing for the Adelaide Strikers. She also recorded the fastest-ever T20 century in women's cricket while playing in the 2015-16 season for the Strikers, doing so in just 36 balls! In addition, she shares the record of winning 23 Player of the Match awards and the highest number of maximums in the history of the competition. 123 of them in all!

BEN STOKES

Full Name: Benjamin Andrew Stokes

Nickname: Stokesy

Born: 4th June, 1991

Born in: Christchurch, New Zealand

Nationality: English

Role: All-rounder

Teams: England, Durham, Melbourne Renegades, Rising Pune Supergiant, Canterbury, Rajasthan Royals, Northern Superchargers, Chennai Super Kings.

One of the most popular English cricket players right now is a man who was born in New Zealand. Ben Stokes moved to England with his parents as a young child. Despite leaving school with very few qualifications, the local cricket teams saw potential in him, and Stokes stayed in England even after his parents moved back to Christchurch. He made history by taking the wicket of experienced former England international player Mark Ramprakash with just his third delivery in professional cricket.

Stokes quickly ascended to the national English team and has been consistently playing for them since 2011. He has become known for delivering exceptional performances that have turned games on their heads. During a Test match against South Africa in Cape Town, Stokes was able to secure 258 runs and take multiple wickets, leading to a famous English win. He has also been largely credited as the driving force behind England's one-wicket win at Headingley Stadium in the 2019 Ashes series by scoring 135 runs without being dismissed!

Now, with 18 centuries scored across both Test and ODI cricket, he is regarded as one of the best all-rounders to play for England. He scored 52 runs in the T20 World Cup final in 2022 as England defeated Pakistan to lift the trophy. In addition, he was also named in the 2019 Cricket World Cup best team, another competition that England won with Stokes in the squad.

MEG LANNING

Full Name: Meghann Moira Lanning

Nickname: Megastar

Born: 25th March, 1992

Born in: Singapore

Nationality: Australian

Role: Batter

Teams: Australia, Victoria, Melbourne Stars, IPL Supernovas, Perth Scorchers, Delhi Capitals

The Singapore-born Australian Meg Lanning has been one of the most consistent performers for her national team and can be relied upon even in high-pressure situations because of her exceptional mental toughness. After winning two World Cups and five T20 World Cups with Australia, she's one of the most decorated female cricketers in the game.

Lanning enjoyed a prolific three-year period between 2014 and 2016, a time in which Australia was the best women's cricket nation. Firstly, she scored 126 runs in the 2014 T20 World Cup final, when Australia won the championship ahead of the West Indies in the final. She would then star in the 2015 Ashes, where her 173 runs in the Test match helped the team retain the trophy.

In November 2023, she announced her retirement from international cricket to focus on her domestic game. Despite all her success with the international team, Lanning has yet to win the Women's Big Bash League in Australia. She is, however, the leading run scorer for the Melbourne Stars, with over 1,800 already in her career!

KEVIN PIETERSEN

Full Name: Kevin Peter Pietersen

Nickname: KP

Born: 27th June, 1980

Born in: Pietermaritzburg, South Africa

Nationality: English

Role: Batter

Teams: England, Natal B, KwaZulu Natal B, KwaZulu Natal, Nottinghamshire, Marylebone, Hampshire, Royal Challengers Bangalore, Surrey, Dolphins, Delhi Daredevils, St Lucia Stars, Melbourne Stars, Quetta Gladiators, Rising Pune Supergiants.

Kevin Pietersen faced adversity in his nation of birth, South Africa, but he played for England because he qualified via his English mother. The batsman is commonly associated with some of the contemporary high points of English cricket, starting with the victorious 2005 Ashes series. In 2008, he made history with England as he scored the ODI fastest century for the national team at the time. He achieved this with just 69 balls at the Oval against South Africa.

His 10-year international career ended with the T20 World Cup in 2010, and he has scored over 8,000 runs for his country in Test cricket. In one of his last games for England, he scored 227 runs in the second Test of the 2010-11 Ashes series. He was later awarded an MBE by the British government for his services to cricket.

Unfortunately, Pietersen hasn't had much success outside of the England national team setup, often finishing in second place with many of his T20 teams like Quetta Gladiators, the Rising Pune Supergiants, and others. He retired from cricket in 2016 and now does charity work, trying to raise awareness of the challenges faced by endangered animals in South Africa.

JOS BUTTLER

Full Name: Joseph Charles Buttler

Born: 8th September, 1990

Hometown: Somerset, England

Nationality: English

Role: Wicketkeeper and Batsman

Teams: England, Somerset, Melbourne Renegades, Lancashire, Mumbai Indians, Comilla Victorians, Sydney Thunder, Rajasthan Royals, Paarl Royals.

Jos Buttler is the captain of the English national team for limited-overs cricket. This wicketkeeper specialist has made multiple key catches and stumpings throughout his career. In addition to those defensive actions, he's also considered a powerful batter who can score runs in good numbers. His skills played a key role in England winning both the 2019 World Cup and the 2022 T20 World Cup.

Buttler has also been very successful in franchise cricket, winning titles in both Bangladesh and India in T20 competitions. His performances in this discipline have led him to be named the ICC's T20I cricketer of the year in 2021. He is widely considered to be one of the best players in short-form cricket.

Buttler has had many stellar career performances. On one occasion, when playing for the Rajasthan Royals, he surpassed the scoring record for an English player in the Indian Premier League, which was previously held by the legendary Jonny Bairstow. He has also played very well at the Rose Bowl in

Southampton, where he scored 144 for Somerset and, at the same ground, hit 152 for England against Pakistan.

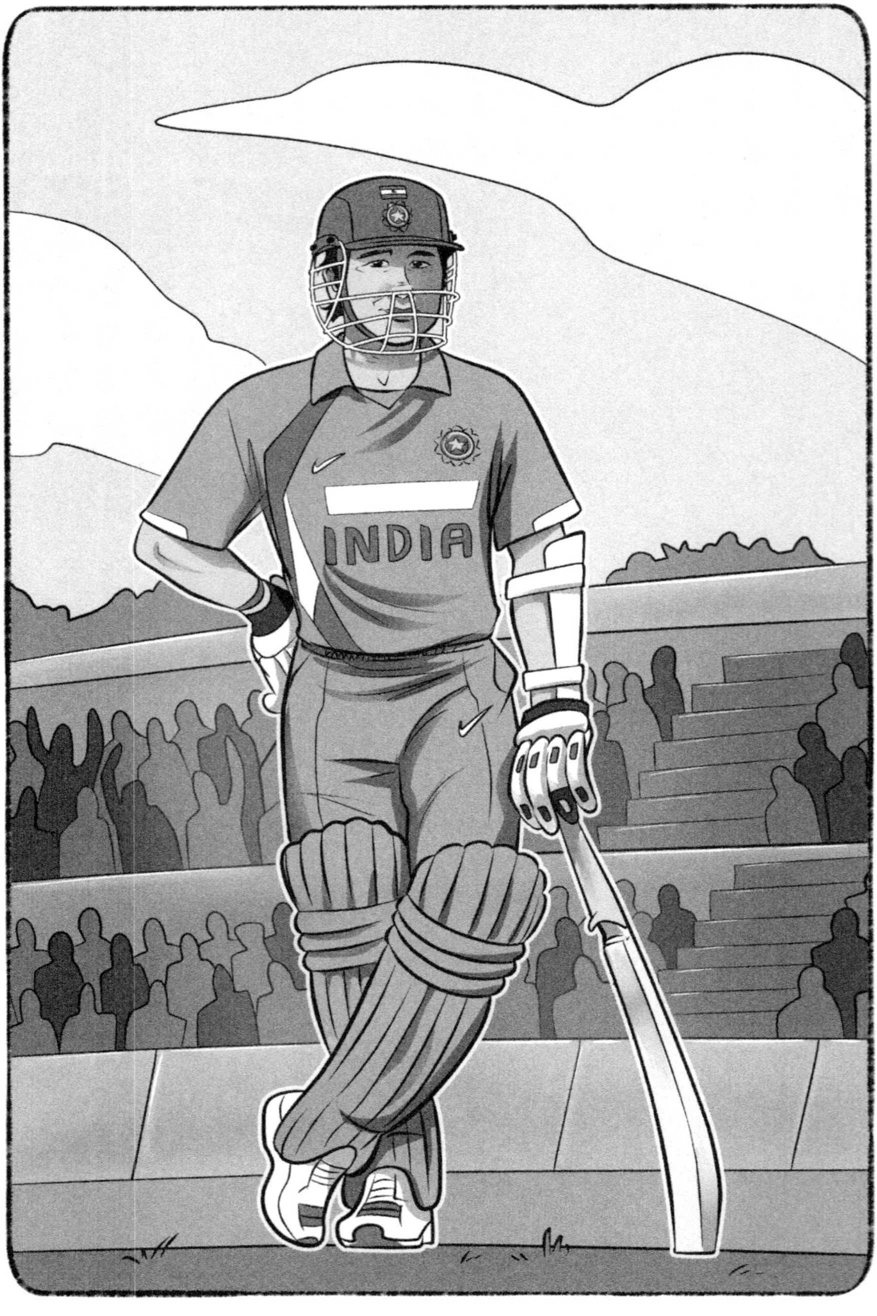
INDIA

SACHIN TENDULKAR

Full Name: Sachin Ramesh Tendulkar

Nickname: Little Master

Born: 24th May, 1973

Hometown: Bombay, India

Nationality: India

Role: Batter

Teams: India, Mumbai, Yorkshire, East Bengal, Mumbai Indians

Sachin Tendulkar is one of the most revered cricket players ever. The Indian batsman played for the national team for over 20 years, from 1989 to 2013. He played the majority of his career in his homeland, with only one short stint in England when he played for Yorkshire in county cricket.

Tendulkar is considered by many Indian cricket fans to be a tenacious and dedicated player. Despite suffering from depression in 2007 and having a very visible decline in form, leading him to be dropped from the T20 World Cup (which India won without him), he still played himself back into the team, playing until he reached the age of 40.

One of his best-ever performances came at Sydney Cricket Ground in 2004 in a Test match against Australia. His 241 score on the day has often been sensationalised as a cricket masterclass. Seven years later, he was still performing at the highest level for India, finishing as the second top run-scorer with 482 runs in the 2011 World Cup, when India triumphed in the tournament.

As well as his long-standing dedication to the national team, Little Master was also a fine servant to the Indian Premier League, playing for the Mumbai Indians for the entirety of his T20 franchise career. When he left the sport, he retired as the fifth highest-scoring player in the competition, with 2,334 runs. As a sign of respect, the Mumbai Indians retired his famous number 10 jersey in tribute to him. His respect goes beyond the cricket field, as Tendulkar served in the Indian government for many years after he retired from professional sport.

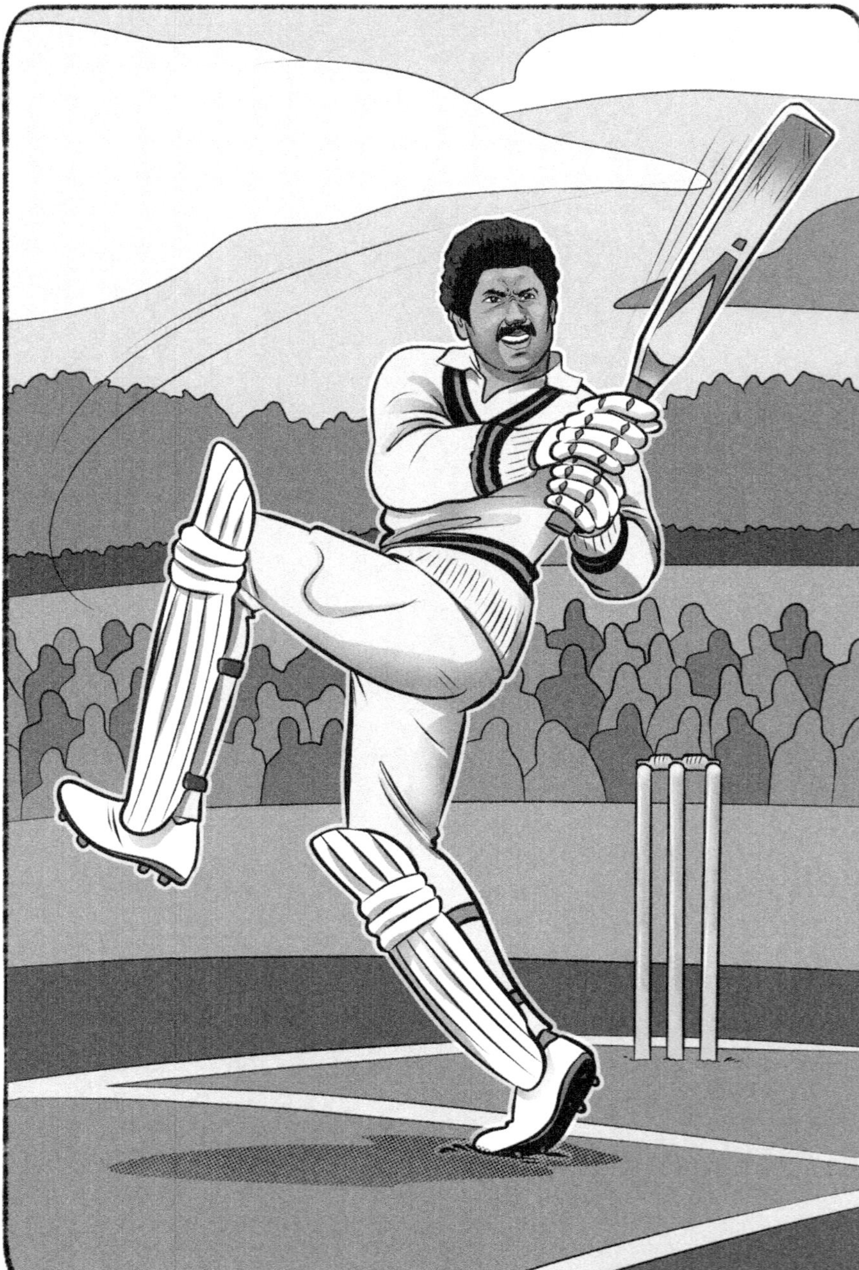

KAPIL DEV

Full Name: Kapil Dev Nikhanj

Born: 6th January, 1959

Hometown: Chandigarh, India

Nationality: Indian

Role: All-rounder

Teams: India, Haryana, Northamptonshire, Worcestershire

For many Indian cricket fans, Kapil Dev is the very definition of an all-rounder. Throughout his career, he scored over 5,000 runs and took 400 wickets in Test cricket, making him one of the country's most efficient players in both aspects of the game. His most famous career moment was in the 1983 Cricket World Cup in England, where he captained the team to success. While he only scored 15 runs in the final against the West Indies, he amassed 303 throughout the entire tournament, helping the team lift the trophy at Lord's in London. 175 of those runs came in a group-stage match against Zimbabwe, a game which India was projected to lose before Dev took to the field.

In 2010, Dev was inducted into the ICC Cricket Hall of Fame, and he was honoured with multiple accolades from the Indian government for his services to cricket while representing his country. He also appeared in an English county cricket competition with two different teams but didn't have nearly as much success at this level.

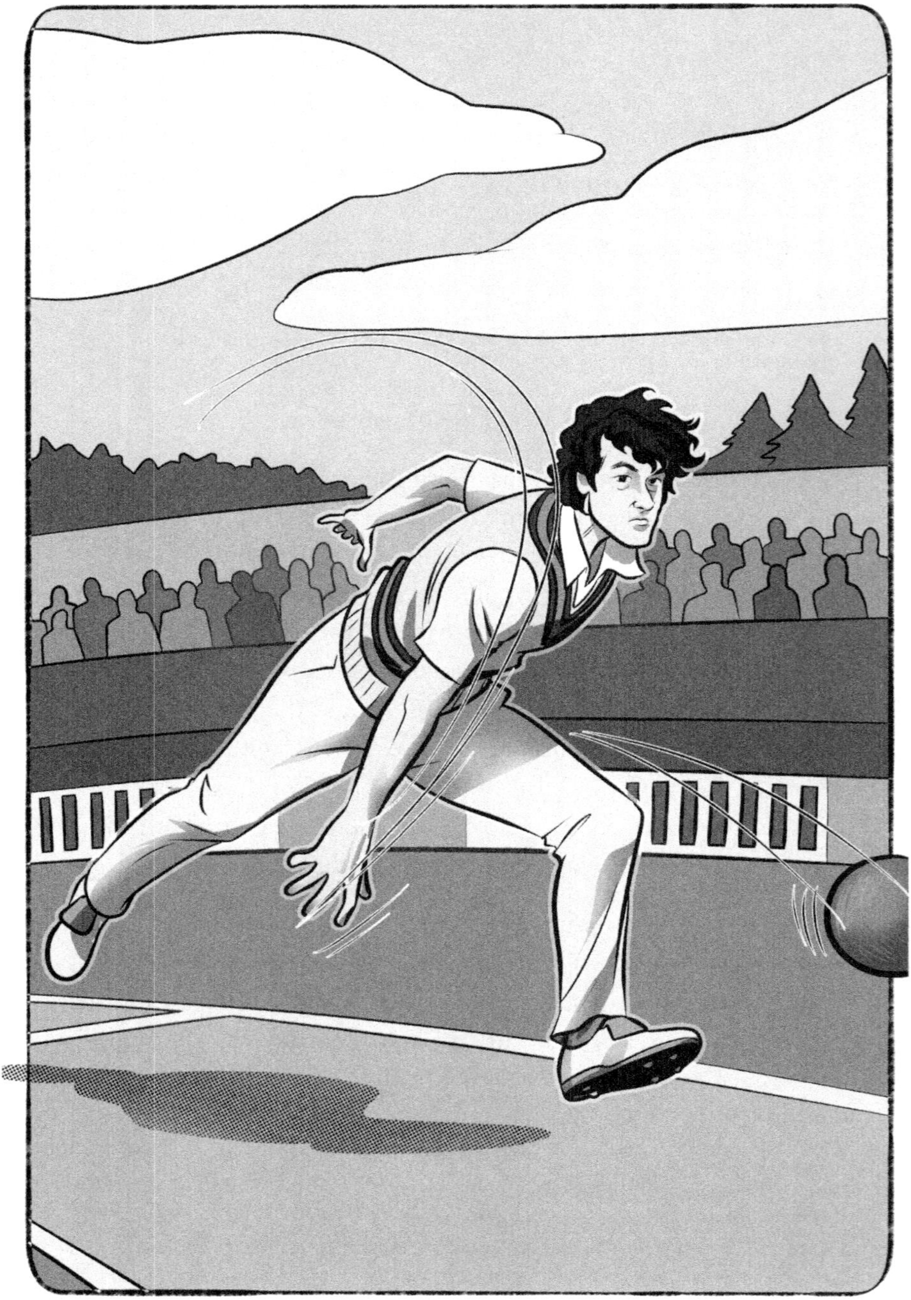

IMRAN KHAN

Full Name: Imran Ahmad Khan Niazi

Nickname: Captain

Born: 5th October, 1952

Hometown: Lahore, Pakistan

Nationality: Pakistani

Role: All-rounder

Teams: Pakistan, Lahore, Worcestershire, Sussex.

How many cricket players can say they've played for their country and also led it as their prime minister? Imran Khan is such a person! Khan played for Pakistan for over 20 years, but one of his finest moments came toward the end of his career at the 1992 Cricket World Cup in Australia. Pakistan played England in the final at the famous Melbourne Cricket Ground when Khan rose to the occasion. In his last-ever ODI match, he scored 72 runs, which helped his nation lift the trophy.

That, however, wasn't the first time Khan had excelled in Melbourne. In the 1981-82 Test series between Pakistan and Australia, Khan bowled 11 wickets (six in the first innings and then five in the second), allowing the Australians to score only 102 runs in the process. Khan's bowling throughout the series proved to be very important to his nation's success.

In addition to his successes with Pakistan, he tasted victory in English county cricket in 1974, when he helped Worcestershire to the County Championship. He also won competitions during his time with Sussex in the 1980s.

After retiring from cricket, Khan was quick to enter politics, founding his own political party in only four years. He served as the prime minister of Pakistan between 2018 and 2022.

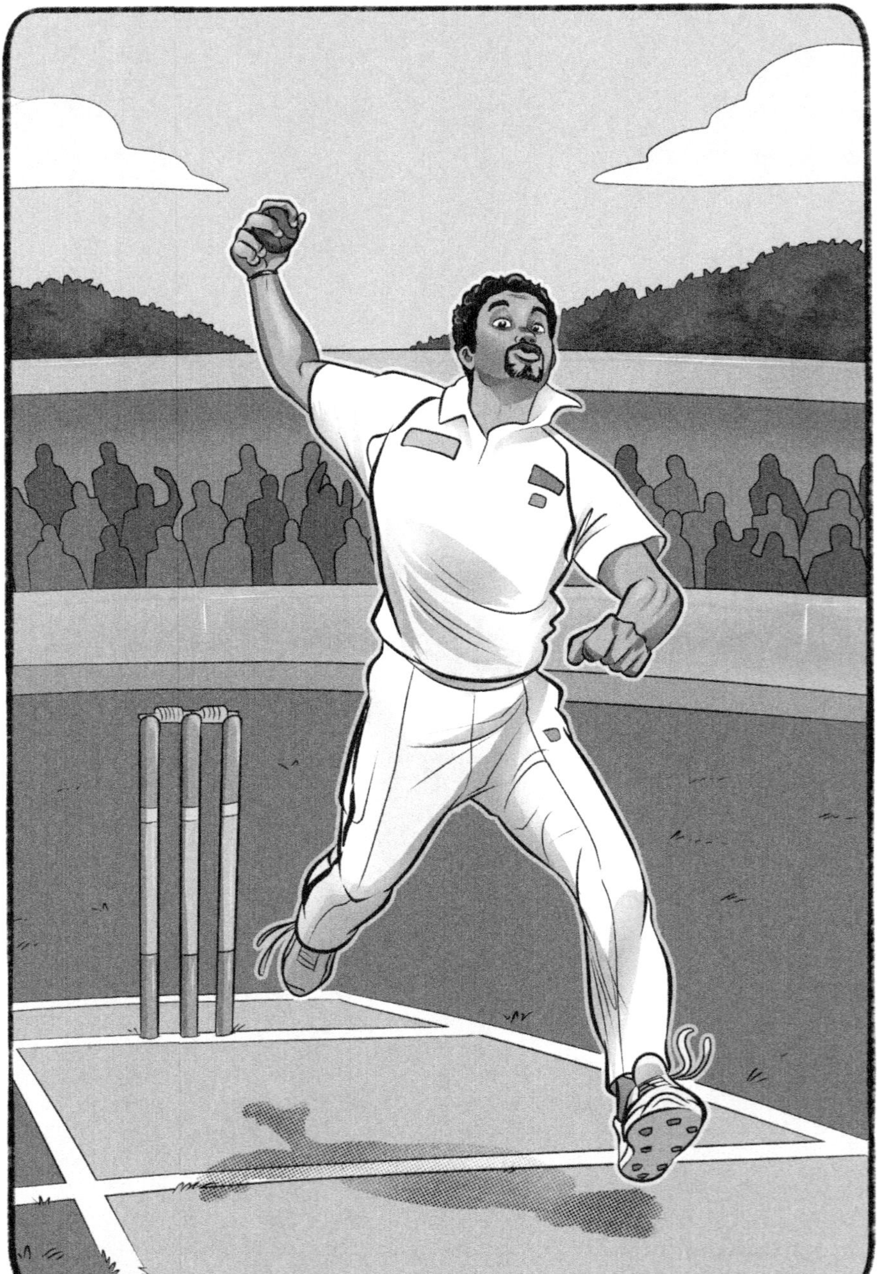

MUTTIAH MURALITHARAN

Full Name: Muttiah Muralitharan

Nickname: Murali

Born: 17th April, 1972

Hometown: Kandy, Ceylon (now known as Sri Lanka)

Nationality: Sri Lankan

Role: Bowler

Teams: Sri Lanka, Tamil Union, Lancashire, Kent, Chennai Super Kings, Kochi Tuskers Kerala, Gloucestershire, Wellington Firebirds, Chittagong Kings, Royal Challengers Bangalore, Melbourne Renegades, Jamaica Tallawahs.

There were a few cricket players who were deemed so good at bowling that the ICC had to change its rules and laws of the game! That is the level of impact that Muttiah Muralitharan had on international cricket. He still holds the record for the highest number of Test cricket wickets, bowling 800 of them. In addition to the record, he also took 534 ODI wickets, another world cricket record.

One of his most memorable performances came in 2002, in a Test match against Zimbabwe in his hometown of Kandy. In this match, he took nine wickets and allowed only 51 runs from the African opposition. This is commonly referred to as one of the best-ever bowling performances in Test cricket. He wasn't just prolific in Test cricket, however, as he proved in the same year when he bowled five wickets in an ODI match against New Zealand, which left the Kiwis with just nine runs on the board.

While Murali was a generational talent who played for the Sri Lankan national cricket team between 1992 and 2011, he only won one major honour with the nation. That came in 1996 when Sri Lanka won the World Cup. He did, however, bulk up his trophy cabinet by winning the Division Two championship in England with Lancashire, the Indian Premier League during his time with the Chennai Super Kings and had success with the Jamaica Tallawahs in the Caribbean Premier League, as well.

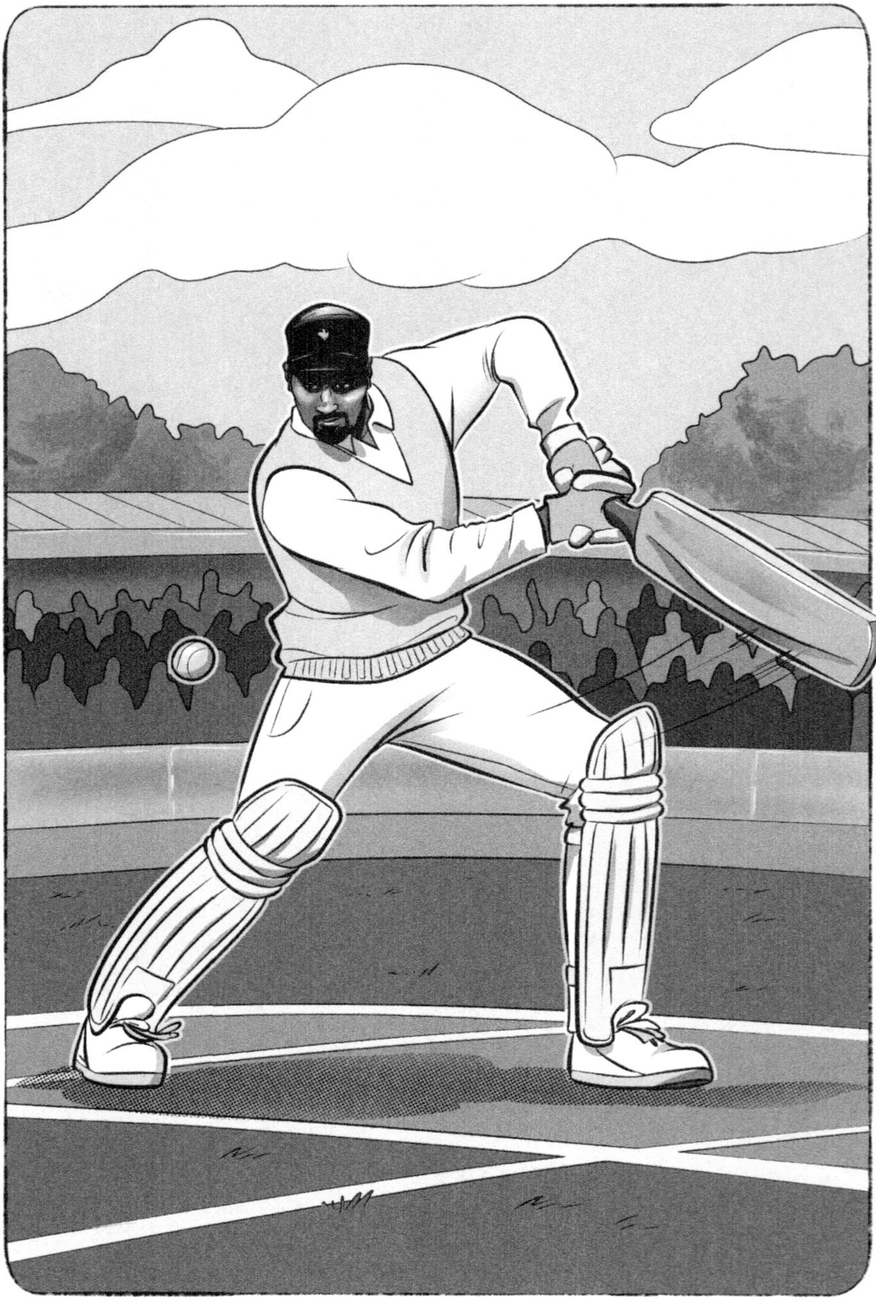

VIV RICHARDS

Full Name: Sir Isaac Vivian Alexander Richards

Nickname: Master Blaster

Born: 7th March, 1952

Hometown: St. John's, Antigua and Barbuda

Nationality: Antiguan

Role: Batter

Teams: West Indies, Combined Islands, Leeward Islands, Somerset, Queensland, Glamorgan.

Viv Richards is one of the most exciting batters in the history of cricket! He played for the West Indies team from 1974 until 1991. In Test cricket, he averaged 50 runs per match, and was considered a top batter. He played an active role in both the 1975 and 1979 Cricket World Cup, which the West Indies both won. In the 1979 tournament, he scored 217 runs, the second-highest by a single player in the tournament. Richards would continue to score consistently for the West Indies, making 24 centuries in Test cricket and another 11 in ODI.

One of his best performances came in 1981 when he scored a double century against England, with a total of 232, while not being dismissed against England in a Test match. He loved playing against the English team, scoring 829 runs in a four-Test series in 1976. He would later rack up a 189 not-out score at Old Trafford in 1984.

The Master Blaster also played in England, appearing for Somerset for 12 years, where he won multiple competitions and tournaments. After retiring from international cricket, Richards played a few seasons for Glamorgan and won a regional tournament in his last-ever season.

As a result of his legacy in cricket, the Sir Vivian Richards Stadium was constructed and named after him in 2012. He has also been named in multiple national honours, and was appointed an OBE from the British government and a Knight Commander from his native Antigua.

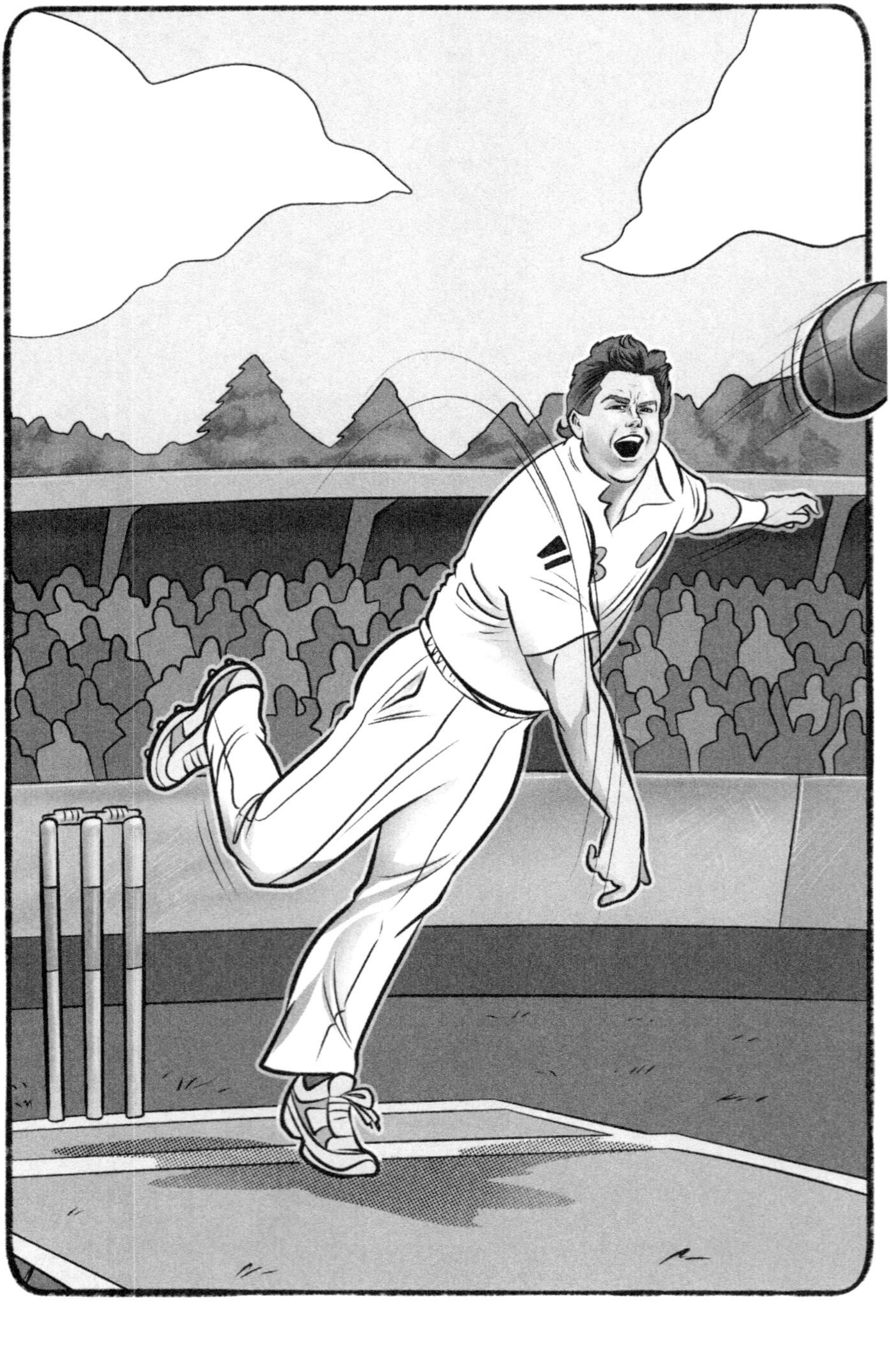

SHANE WARNE

Full Name: Shane Keith Warne

Born: 13th September, 1969

Nickname: The King of Spin

Died: 4th March, 2022

Hometown: Victoria, Australia

Nationality: Australian

Role: Bowler

Teams: Australia, Victoria, Hampshire, Rajasthan Royals, Melbourne Stars.

Affectionately known as the King of Spin, Shane Warne was a superstar bowler in every team he played for. However, it was the Australian national team for which he is best remembered. In 1999, he took 20 wickets, the joint-top throughout the entirety of the tournament, as the Australians won the championship. This included a heroic performance in the final at Lord's, where he took four wickets against Pakistan.

After winning the World Cup in 1999, Warne went from strength to strength, proving to be one of the best bowlers in international cricket during this era. This included taking 31 wickets in the 2001 Ashes series, taking 40 in the 2005 edition and helping Australia regain the trophy in the 2006-07 series in his last-ever involvement in the competition. However, some cricket fans believe that his debut appearance in the Ashes back in 1993 was his best, as he delivered the 'Ball of the Century', dismissing Mike Gatting and finishing the series with 34 wickets.

Warne also won multiple titles in domestic cricket, lifting the Sheffield Shield with Victoria multiple times. He also made Indian Premier League history when he served as the Rajasthan Royals captain in 2008 when the team won the championship title.

After retiring from his playing career, Warne often commented on cricket matches. Tragically, in 2022, Shane Warne passed away at the age of just 52. He was on holiday with his family in Thailand when he suffered a fatal heart attack. In honour and tribute to Warne, a state memorial event took place at Melbourne Cricket Ground in March 2023.

KAREN ROLTON

Full Name: Karen Louise Rolton

Born: 21st November, 1974

Hometown: Adelaide, Australia

Nationality: Australian

Role: Batter

Teams: Australia, South Australia

Karen Rolton is the top female scorer of Test cricket runs in Australian history. Her career spanned from 1995 to 2009, during which period she won the Cricket World Cup in both 1997 and 2005. She was named the player of the tournament and the final in the later edition as she scored 246 runs in an exceptional performance for the Australian team. Unfortunately, the inception of T20 Women's World Cups came a little late for Rolton, as she only played in the first tournament in 2009. She captained the team as they reached the semi-final – but had retired by the time the 2010 competition took place.

In 2001, she put in an inspiring performance at the Test match at Headingley in Leeds, where she recorded an exceptional 209 score and was not dismissed. This allowed her to set up an average batting score of 55 in Test cricket.

Rolton is still very much involved in cricket today, after her playing career, and now works as a coach with the Melbourne Renegades. As an individual, she has been recognised for her exceptional performances, and was inducted into the Sport Australia Hall of Fame in 2021. She was named the ICC female cricketer of the year in 2006.

DEBBIE HOCKLEY

Full Name: Deborah Ann Hockley

Born: 7th November, 1962

Hometown: Christchurch, New Zealand

Nationality: New Zealander

Role: All-rounder

Teams: New Zealand, Canterbury Magicians, North Shore

No other female player has as many runs as Debbie Hockley in the Women's Cricket World Cup. She scored 1,501 runs during appearances in the tournament between 1982 and 2000. It was in her last appearance as a 38-year-old in 2000 when she lifted the Cricket World Cup trophy, when New Zealand won the championship by four runs at Bert Sutcliffe Oval on home soil.

Hockley made multiple centuries across both Test and ODI cricket and subsequently got a batting average of 50 for all disciplines of the sport. One of her most notable performances came in England at the Riverside Ground, where she scored 117 in a One Day International match against the English team in 1996. As an all-rounder and ODI specialist, she was also able to take 20 wickets during her bowling performances from 118 games.

In addition to her fantastic career with the New Zealand national team, Hockley won multiple honours with the Canterbury Magicians and North Shore, who competed at the top level of New Zealand's cricket system. Retired from playing, Hockley is still participating, serving as the president of the New Zealand cricket board in 2016. She was later honoured by her country in the 2021 honours list, when she was named a Companion of the New Zealand Order of Merit.

EOIN MORGAN

Full Name: Eoin Joseph Gerard Morgan

Born: 10th September, 1986

Nickname: Captain Morgan

Hometown: Dublin, Ireland

Nationality: Irish and English

Role: Batter

Teams: Ireland, England, Middlesex, Royal Challengers Bangalore, Kolkata Knight Riders, Gazi Tank Cricketers, Sydney Thunder, Sunrisers Hyderabad, Peshawar Zalmi, Kings XI Punjab, Barbados Tridents, Karachi Kings, Tshwane Spartans, London Spirit.

Eoin Morgan might have been born in Dublin, Ireland, but has since become an English cricket hero. The middle-order batsman initially played for Ireland's national cricket team between 2006 and 2009 but qualified to switch nations due to his English mother. Morgan has openly admitted that from the age of 13, his goal was always to play for England, given that the sport is much more followed there than it is in Ireland. It was a dream realised when he was named in the T20 World Cup squad for England in 2010. He would go on to score 183 runs in the tournament as England won when they defeated Australia in the final. Morgan was also integral to the 2019 team that won the Cricket World Cup on home soil.

Interestingly, Morgan has played on both sides of the fixture between Ireland and England. Early in his career, he went to the 2007 Cricket World Cup with Ireland. The underdog team made it to the Super Eight phase. Morgan would be bowled out with only two runs by Sajid Mahmood, who would later be his teammate in the England camp.

Morgan has also had an extensive career in domestic cricket, playing for a wealth of different teams. He has won multiple Indian Premier League titles with both the Sunrisers Hyderabad and the Kolkata Knight Riders. His trophy cabinet needed to be expanded when he won T20 tournaments in both Pakistan and Australia. In addition, he helped Middlesex win one County Championship back in 2016.

At the end of 2023, Eoin Morgan stated that he would be retiring from all forms of cricket. He is now more focused on his media career, and works with sports TV companies as a cricket commentator. He has been praised and recognised for his services to cricket and has been given a CBE by the British government.

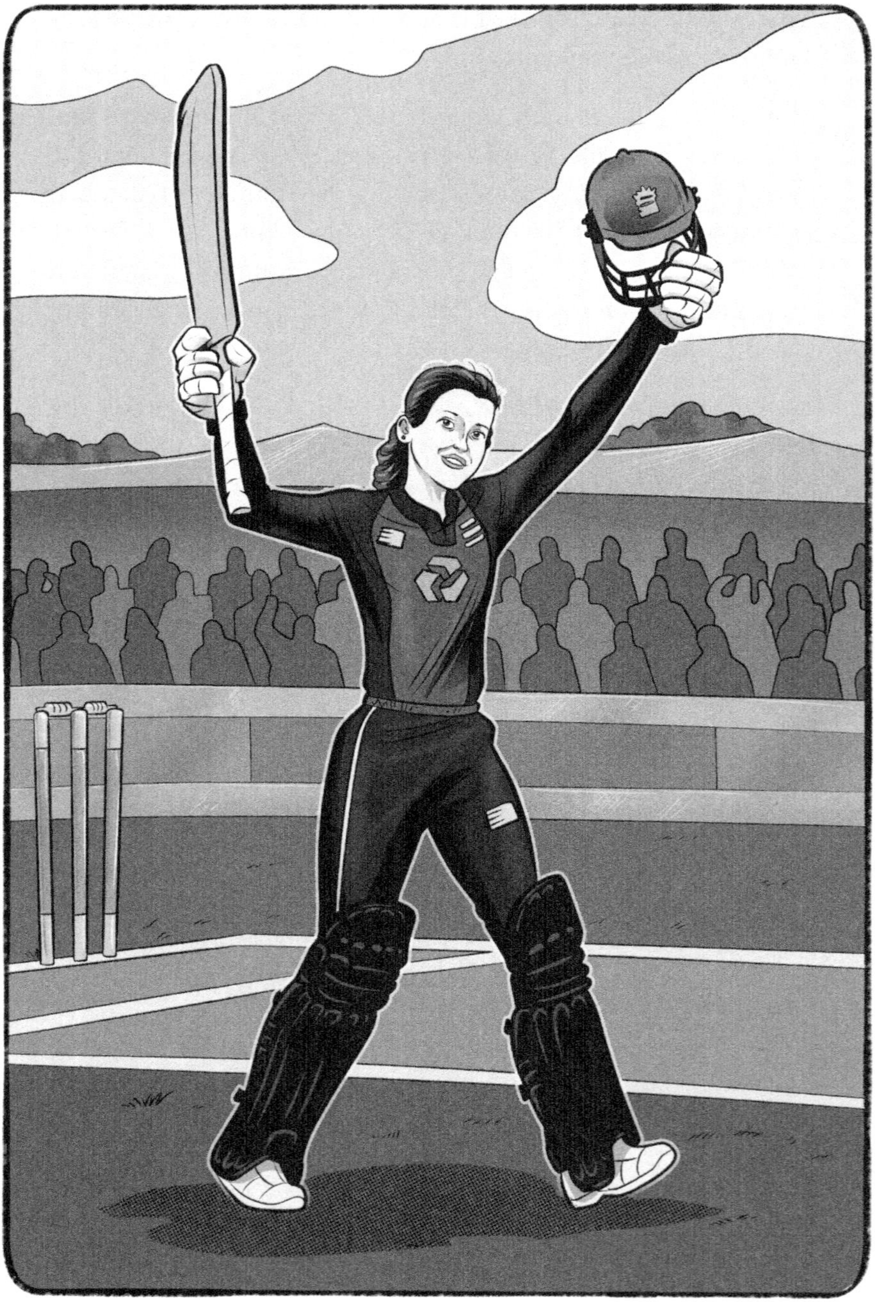

SARAH TAYLOR

Full Name: Sarah Jane Taylor

Born: 20th May, 1989

Hometown: London, England

Nationality: England

Role: Wicketkeeper and Batter

Teams: England, Sussex, Wellington, South Australian Scorpions, Adelaide Strikers, Lancashire Thunder, Surrey Stars, Northern Diamonds, Welsh Fire.

Three-time ICC cricketer of the year, Sarah Taylor, has been a prominent part of English cricket since arriving in the team in 2006. Before Taylor's involvement, the team had finished in the semi-finals at the 2005 World Cup. In 2009, with her on the squad, England won the entire tournament. Sarah was named within the overall best eleven for the entire tournament as the wicketkeeper. She played a starring role in the final against New Zealand as she batted first and ran a score of 39 to start the innings.

After that initial period of success for England and Taylor, she was part of the T20 World Cup success, also in 2009, and then many years later in the 2017 Cricket World Cup. In fact, in 2017, she was able to score 396 runs throughout the tournament. In that final against India, Taylor scored 45 runs, as England won the championship by nine runs.

In addition to her stellar career with the English national team, the wicketkeeper also played for multiple domestic teams in England, Australia and New Zealand. She picked up trophies with the Surrey Stars, the South Australian Scorpions, and County Cricket wins with Sussex.

Taylor is still very active in cricket, saying that even though she hasn't played professionally since 2021, she hasn't ruled out a return to the sport. She currently works with the men's team at Sussex as a wicketkeeper coach (making history by becoming the first woman to be appointed as a coach on a men's team) and as an assistant coach at the Manchester Originals for both male and female teams in the Hundred competition.

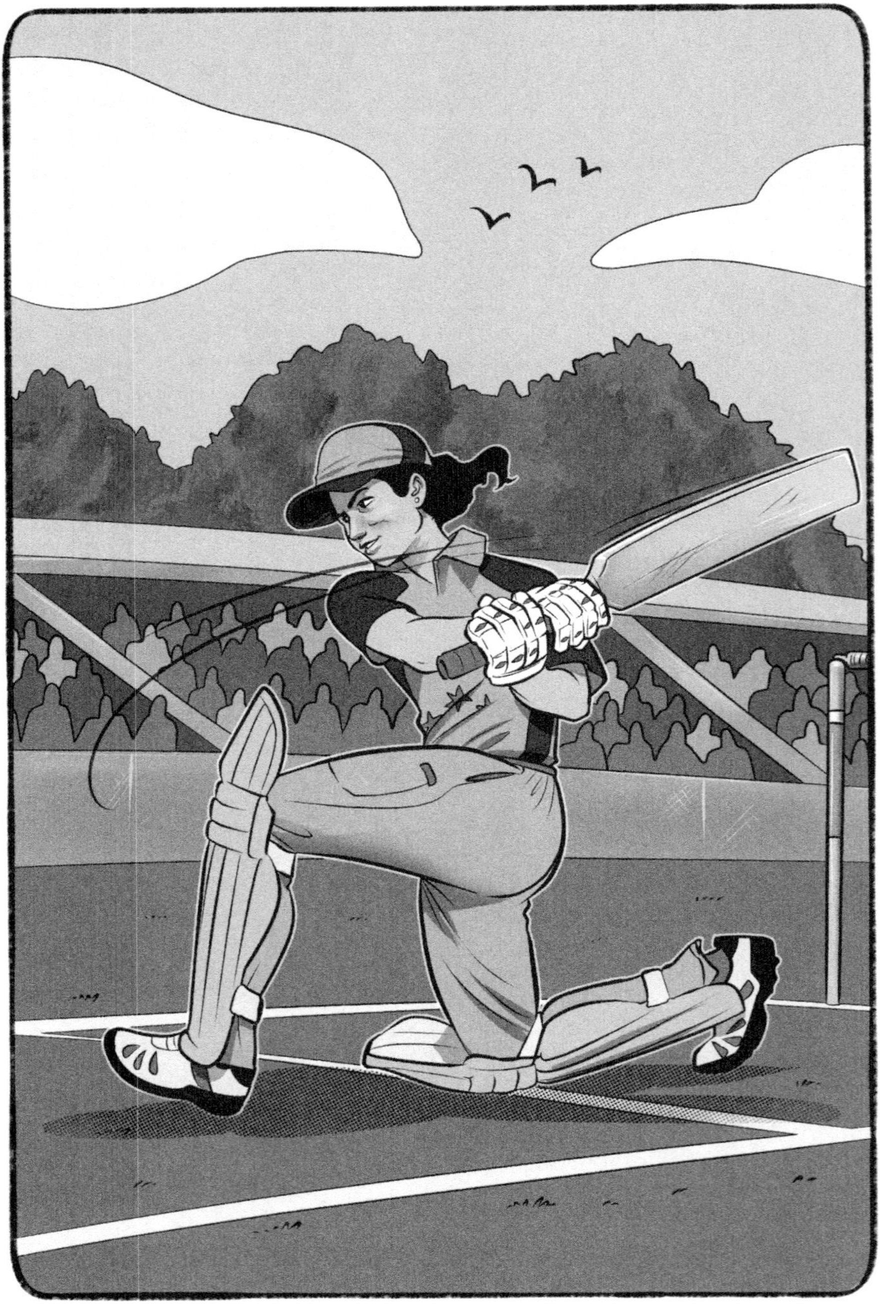

LISA STHALEKAR

Full Name: Lisa Carprini Sthalekar

Nickname: Shaker

Born: 13th August, 1979

Born in: Pune, India

Nationality: Australian

Role: All-rounder

Teams: Australia, New South Wales, Sydney Sixers

Lisa Sthalekar had quite a journey from her humble beginnings in an orphanage in Pune, India, to becoming the captain of the Australian national team. One of the most consistent all-round performers, she was the first woman to score 1,000 runs and take 100 wickets in ODI cricket. She was part of both national teams that won the 2005 and 2013 Cricket World Cup. Throughout her career, she recorded three international centuries, one against her nation of birth, India, in Sydney, the city she emigrated to.

In domestic cricket, Sthalekar enjoyed many years with the New South Wales Breakers, triumphing in the Women's National Cricket League. In franchise T20 cricket, she played for the Sydney Sixers in the Women's Big Bash League. Now retired from the game completely, she has worked as a commentator for Australian coverage of various cricket competitions.

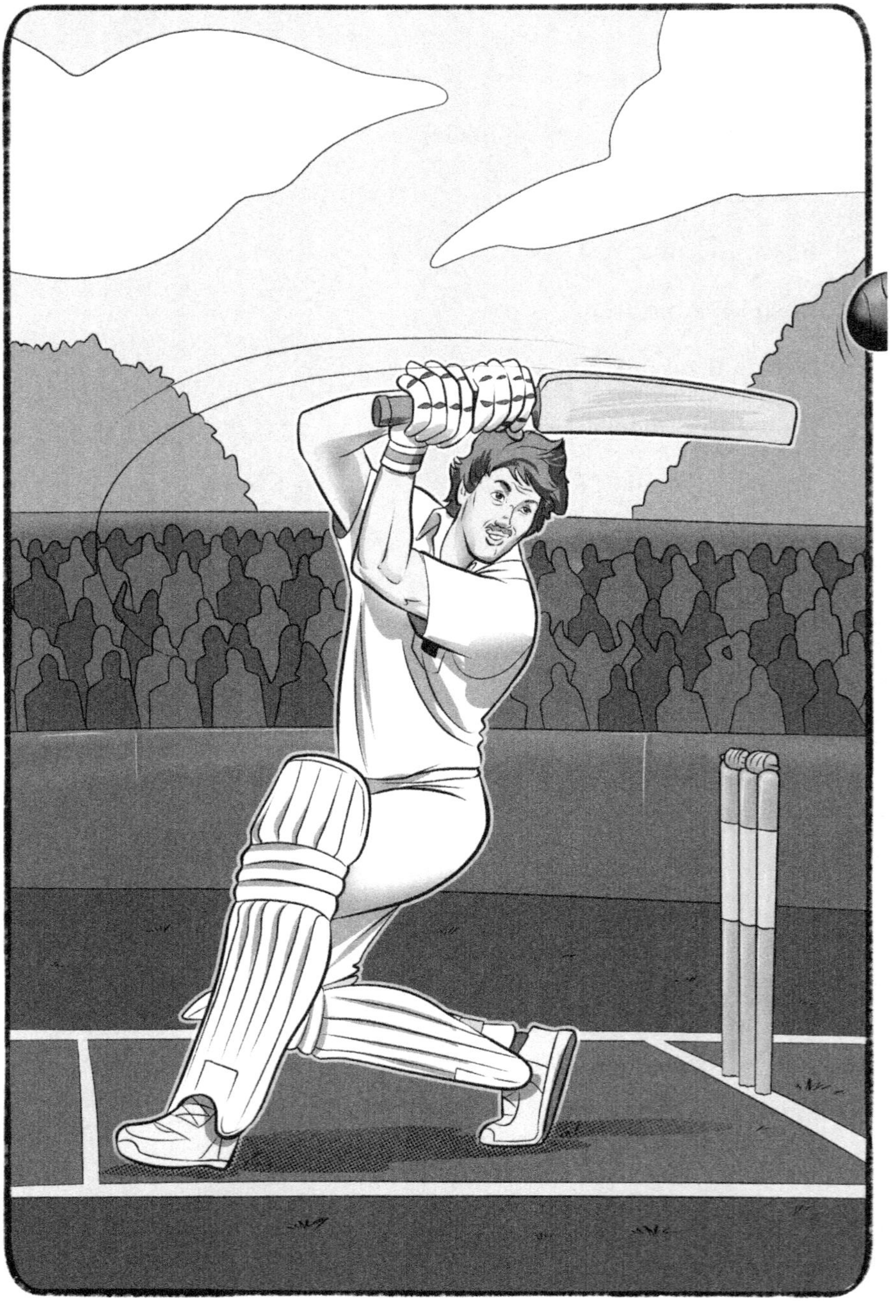

IAN BOTHAM

Full Name: Ian Terence Botham, Baron Botham

Born: 24th November, 1955

Nickname: Both

Hometown: Cheshire, England

Nationality: English

Role: All-rounder

Teams: England, Somerset, Queensland, Worcestershire, Durham

Ian Botham is one of the greatest cricketers to have played the game, not just in England but in the entire world of international cricket. Ahead of England's 1000th Test match in August 2018, the England Cricket Board revealed its greatest squad of all time, with Ian Botham among the names on the team. Botham never won a major international tournament with England but was a key figure in the years that the team finished second. In the 1992 tournament, he famously took 16 wickets, which was the joint top in the competition.

Despite not winning a trophy with England, Botham still enjoyed a long career in English County cricket, playing with Somerset, Worcestershire and Durham. He also spent one season in Australia, playing with Queensland.

Botham was a very talented sportsman, playing football at school along with cricket. In the 1970s and 80s, Botham refused to give up football and decided to make himself available to Yeovil Town, who played him as a defender. At certain points of the season, fans could see an England international cricketer playing a completely different sport! He would transfer to Scunthorpe United but made very few appearances and ultimately retired from football in 1985 to focus on his cricket.

After retiring from cricket in the 1990s, Botham worked as a commentator for cricket coverage in the UK and enjoyed critical acclaim for his success in analysing the game. In the 2020s, the former cricket player briefly served in the UK government.

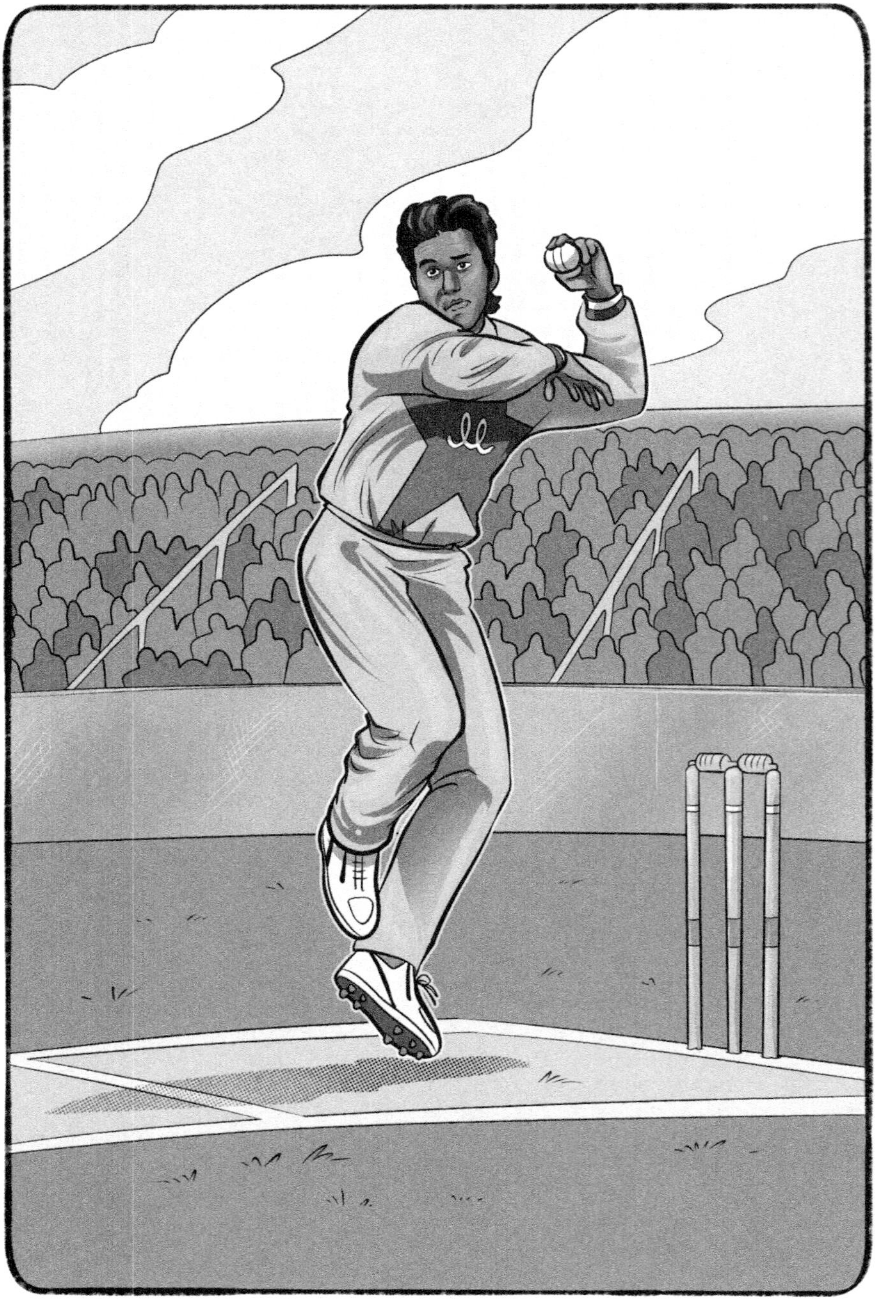

WASIM AKRAM

Full Name: Wasim Akram

Born: 3rd June, 1966

Nickname: Sultan of Swing

Hometown: Lahore, Pakistan

Nationality: Pakistani

Role: All-rounder

Teams: Pakistan, Lahore, Lancashire, PIA, Hampshire.

Wasim Akram is a celebrated all-round cricketer who specializes in fast-bowling techniques. For almost 20 years, he played for Pakistan, as the nation became one of the most highly-rated countries in international cricket. He became the first-ever bowler to reach the 500-wicket milestone in ODI cricket, doing so in the 2003 World Cup.

His finest hour for Pakistan arguably came in 1992 in the Cricket World Cup, as his 18 wickets throughout the tournament took the team to the championship title, beating England in the final at Melbourne Cricket Ground. Akram was named the man of the match as he took three wickets and scored 33 runs, which ensured a win for his nation. In addition to his international cricket, Akram played a lot of cricket in the English county system with both Lancashire and Hampshire.

Following his cricket career, Akram embarked on other career paths tailored to his interests in books, modelling, business and both television and film industries. He has also worked on multiple charitable causes to raise awareness of diabetes. He has since returned to cricket in administrative duties, serving in different roles in franchises, including Islamabad United, the Multan Sultans and the Karachi Kings.

RICHARD HADLEE

Full Name: Sir Richard John Hadlee

Born: 3rd July, 1951

Hometown: St Albans, New Zealand

Nationality: New Zealander

Role: All-rounder

Teams: Nottinghamshire, Canterbury, Tasmania

Richard Hadlee is one of New Zealand's most revered sportsmen. The all-rounder was named the country's sportsperson of the year on multiple occasions and was even inducted into the ICC Cricket Hall of Fame in 2009. He became the first-ever player to complete the feat of scoring 1,000 runs and bowling 100 wickets in ODI cricket.

While considered an all-rounder, some cricket fans point out that Hadlee was a superb bowler with a fantastic fast-ball technique, which frightened players on the other team. One of his finest periods came in the 1983 Cricket World Cup when he took 14 wickets. Unfortunately, that year New Zealand did not make it out of the group stage.

Hadlee was able to taste success on the cricket pitch in English county cricket, where he played for Nottinghamshire between 1978 and 1987. Throughout this time, he was voted as the player of the year on three different occasions, owing to his exceptional bowling record, often taking around 100 wickets per year. Hadlee also enjoyed moderate success in domestic cricket back in New Zealand while playing for Canterbury.

GRAHAM GOOCH

Full Name: Graham Alan Gooch

Nickname: Goochie

Born: 23rd July, 1953

Hometown: Essex, England

Nationality: English

Role: Batter

Teams: England, Essex, Western Province.

Graham Gooch has been called one of the most influential and hard-working England cricket captains to have represented the nation in both Test and ODI disciplines. He played on the team for 20 years, between 1975 and 1995, up until the age of 42. He took his place in the ICC Cricket Hall of Fame after he scored over 100 centuries at the top level of cricket.

Gooch would often serve as the opening batsman for England as his high-scoring stints would set a good tone for England to win matches. He went to four Cricket World Cups with England, making the finals twice and semi-finals two other times. While they didn't win, he left the 1987 World Cup as the top scorer with 471 runs.

One of Gooch's most prolific performances came in Test cricket against India at Lord's in London in 1990. He scored 333 runs in a Player-of-the-Match performance. His best outing in One Day International cricket was in 1987, when he scored an impressive 142 runs against Pakistan in Karachi. At the height of his fame in the early 1990s, a video game was released called *Graham Gooch World Class Cricket*.

In domestic cricket, Gooch represented Essex in the county competition. During his 24-year career with the team, he won six County Championships and became a local legend to the club. He also played two seasons in South Africa with Western Province, where he enjoyed moderate success.

After retiring from the game in 1997, he first became a commentator for several organizations, but soon found himself a coach at Essex and then later took a lead role as the batting coach with the England team.

4

THE MOST AMAZING GAMES OF CRICKET

While every game of cricket can be exciting and entertaining, there are some famous matches that have become well-known for being some of the greatest cricket games of all time. Whether they were very close or featured some amazing individual performances, I want to share with you some of the best cricket matches ever, so let's get started!

THE IRISH UPSET THE ENGLISH

The M. Chinnaswamy Stadium in Bangalore, India, witnessed not just cricket history in 2011 but sporting history. India was co-hosting the tournament, along with Sri Lanka and Bangladesh. The England team, however, were considered one of the favourites after retaining the Ashes against Australia and winning the T20 World Cup in 2010. They were expected to challenge for the trophy in the 2011 Cricket World Cup.

England started well by defeating the Netherlands but then had a wobble against the hosts, tying the match. Then, they played Ireland. The Irish had lost their last match by a large margin, and because cricket was not nearly as popular as it was in England, they were expected to roll over for England.

Jonathan Trott and Ian Bell scored over 170 runs between them, with other players like Andrew Strauss and Kevin Pietersen pitching in to reach 327 runs. John Mooney, on the other team, bowled nine overs and took four wickets in an impressive performance, which famously took out Paul Collingwood before he could make an impact on the match.

The script was initially followed by the Irish as the captain, William Porterfield, was dismissed before he could score a single run. The English fielders and bowlers could not account for the heroics of Kevin O'Brien, a middle-order batsman who scored 113 runs! He also achieved the quickest century in Cricket World Cup history in just 50 balls. Alex Cusack and John Mooney also put in good performances, which ensured that they reached 328 runs to win the match by three wickets! Graeme Swann tried his best to get wickets for the English, but it wasn't enough, and Ireland secured a rare victory on the international stage.

Ireland, however, didn't win enough games to progress to the knockout stage. While they went home after the group fixtures, they took away the memory of this historic win over the English team. England did advance to the next round but was knocked out by Sri Lanka in the quarter-final.

INDIA END AUSTRALIA'S 26-MATCH WINNING STREAK

Between 2018 and 2021, the Australian women's cricket team were undoubtedly the best ODI cricket team in the world. Players like Beth Mooney, Tahlia McGrath and Nicola Carey allowed them to continually win games, 26 of them in fact. That all came to an end when they played India in their third ODI of 2021. Australia had already won the series but then Jhulan Goswami took three wickets in stellar style while Yastika Bhatia was in great run-scoring form. India won by two wickets to end the Australians winning streak.

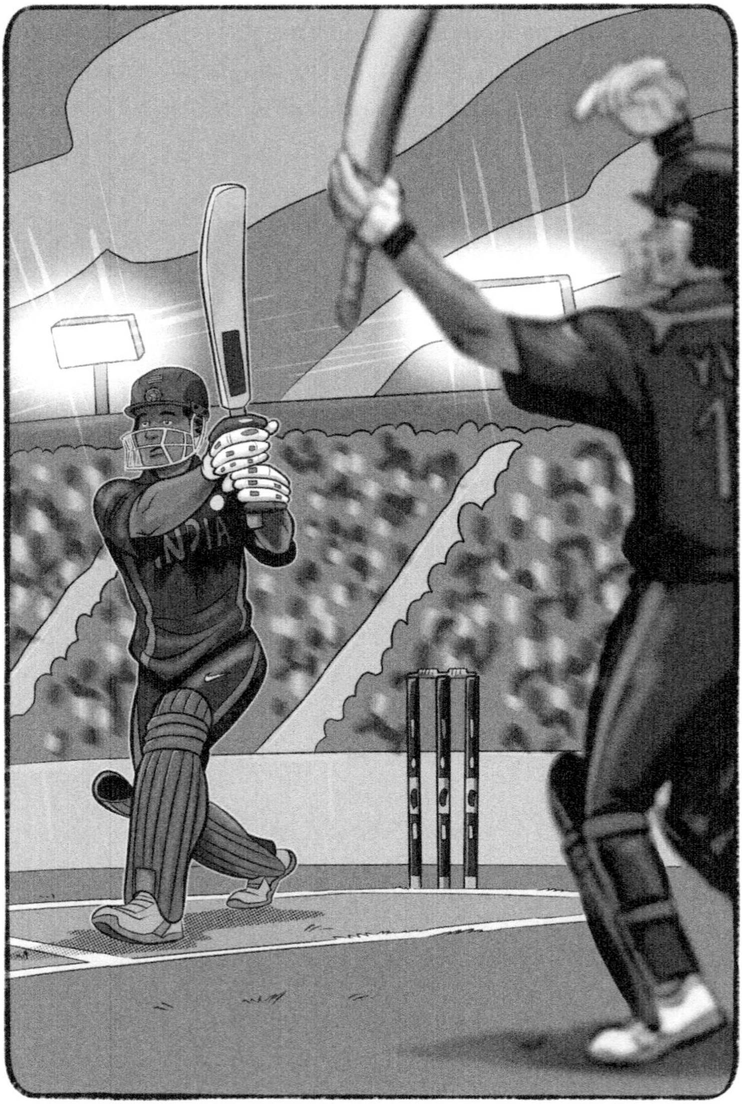

THE 2011 CRICKET WORLD CUP FINAL

The 2011 Cricket World Cup was a marvellous occasion, with three different hosts, two of them making it to the final. India, Sri Lanka and Bangladesh all played their part, with venues from each country holding games from the tournament. India, as the biggest country, had the most venues and held the final at Wankhede Stadium in Mumbai. India had already defeated some of the biggest teams to make it this far, with Australia and Pakistan both sent home by the Indian team. Meanwhile, Sri Lanka enjoyed great form in the tournament, defeating England and New Zealand to reach the finals.

Upul Tharanga didn't start well for Sri Lanka in the batting, scoring just two runs before Zaheer Khan dismissed him. However, after he left the field, Sri Lanka's batter suddenly became very successful. Tillakaratne Dilshan and Kumar Sangakkara got it started with over 80 runs between them. Then Mahela Jayawardene raised the level of play, scoring 103 runs. He did that over 88 balls and was not dismissed as the innings ended. This gave Sri Lanka 274 runs and real hope that they could take the Cricket World Cup trophy back to their homeland.

Much like Sri Lanka, India started their batting very poorly. Virender Sehwag was dismissed after facing just two balls, and scored no runs. Sachin Tendulkar got them off the starting blocks with 18, but it wasn't until Gautam Gambhir took to the field that the team began to threaten to win the game. Gambhir played the long game and scored 97 runs before being bowled out by Thisara Perera.

At the end of the game, it was the partnership of Mahendra Singh Dhoni and Yuvraj Singh that stood tall for India. They were resilient and kept scoring to eventually catch up with the run count. They made 277 runs and won by six wickets, with ten balls remaining. This game was a close contest between the batting strengths, but ultimately, India had the better players across both areas of play and won the trophy. By meeting and passing the 274-run target, they had set the record for the highest successful run chase in a World Cup final.

AUSTRALIA SHOW BRILLIANCE AGAINST DENMARK IN 1997 CRICKET WORLD CUP

Back in 1997, Australia were the team to beat in women's cricket. They were difficult to match, because they had many superstars on their team, like Belinda Clarke, Bronwyn Calver and Karen Rolton, who set a high standard. They entered the 1997 Cricket World Cup in India as one of the favourites, having won it three times previously.

They were placed alongside England, South Africa, Ireland, Pakistan and Denmark in Group A. Denmark is not a country commonly associated with cricket, but it was this match against the Danes that will be remembered for its many records.

Belinda Clarke decided to bat first for Australia; as the captain, she wanted to set a good example for the team. She was able to score consistently throughout all the overs she faced, as she made 229 runs from 155 balls. This was very bad for the Danish bowlers, because they couldn't get her out of the game. She wasn't dismissed at any point. The Denmark captain, Dorte Christiansen, was eventually able to take two wickets, but she and her fellow bowlers couldn't stop Clarke from scoring throughout the 50 overs. Lisa Keightley and Karen Rolton added another 124 runs between themselves to take their score to 412.

Denmark, a team that made its World Cup debut in 1993 (losing six of their seven games in that tournament), would now have to produce a history-making performance to defeat the three-time World Cup champions. History would be made, just not to Denmark's liking.

Dorte Christensen managed to get nine runs, which was the highest score from any member of the Denmark team in the game. The team were clearly out of their depth, as ten of them were dismissed within 26 overs, calling time on the game rather early. In the end, Denmark finished with just 49 runs. Australia won by a margin of 363 runs which is the largest winning margin in a Women's Cricket World Cup. Belinda Clarke's 229 runs is still the highest individual score in the World Cup, and the 412 runs was the highest team score in the competition.

Australia went on to top their group by winning four of their five games (one had no result due to rain). They reached the final, where they would celebrate winning their fourth Women's World Cup championship at Eden Gardens in Calcutta.

Denmark finished the group stage with at least one win, as they defeated Pakistan, but lost their four other games. This meant that they, along with Pakistan, would be exiting the tournament early. Denmark's women's cricket team has not returned to the World Cup since, and has not played ODI cricket since 1999, having won just six of its 33 games. Danish women started to play T20 rules back in 2022, however, with demand for the sport growing.

HISTORY-MAKING FIFTH ODI IN JOHANNESBURG

In 2005 and 2006, Australia played many games against South Africa. The game that everyone remembers from the series even has its own name and is known as the 438 match. Nobody in the New Wanderers Stadium in Johannesburg could have guessed that many cricket records would be broken in this single game. Some cricket fans have even called this the 'greatest ODI match' of all time!

This game was set up very nicely, with both teams having won two of the prior matches, meaning that the winner in this one would win the five-game ODI series. Strangely, both teams were without their superstar bowlers. This could be why all the scoring records were torn apart here. No team had made a 400-run score in an ODI match before, yet both Australia and South Africa changed that.

Australia was first to bat with Adam Craig Gilchrist, who scored an impressive 55 runs. While this was a very good way to set the tone, his partner got even more, as Simon Katich got the team 79 in a very solid start for Australia. Yet, the best performance came from the captain, Ricky Ponting, who managed 164 runs from just 105 balls, hitting nine maximums before being caught out. In the end, Australia ended the innings with a record-breaking 434 runs, which comfortably broke the previous ODI score record of 398 by Sri Lanka from 1996. When the teams were switching over, newspapers and websites were already reporting that there was a new ODI world record!

South Africa took to the field knowing they would also need to put in a record-breaking performance if they were to win the game and the series. Graeme Smith started the innings in good fashion by scoring 90 runs. Yet the country needed a real hero to match Ponting's efforts. Enter Herschelle Gibbs. The batsman took 175 runs in a marvellous performance. Nathan Wade Bracken did his best to stop South Africa from scoring by taking five wickets from his ten overs.

The end of the game was dramatic, as Andrew James Hall was batting for South Africa in the final over of the match. By this point, both teams had already beaten the previous world record, and South Africa believed they could win, needing only seven runs from six balls. He hit a four, which ensured they only needed two more runs. Hall was caught out, leaving the bowler, Makhaya Ntini, as the last man to bat for South Africa. Mark Boucher was still in the game, steadily scoring. In a heroic move, he hit his 50th ODI four-pointer to seal the win for South Africa with 438 runs. Two new world records were made in one match!

ENGLAND WINS BY A SINGLE RUN!

The women's T20 tournament in 2016 was a great tournament, with India hosting the competition. The hosts were placed in Group B, but it was fellow teams in the same group that stole the show here. England and the West Indies produced a very close match on the fourth matchday.

The West Indies batted first. Stefanie Taylor and Shaquana Quintyne scored over 60 runs between them, and the overall team set a very respectable 108 runs on the board. Nat Sciver-Brunt and Anya Shrubsole were the best bowlers for England, allowing the least number of runs for the West Indies.

Charlotte Edwards, as the captain, led by example when England started batting, making 30 runs, along with her partner, Tammy Beaumont, who made 31. The comeback was on! But relatively quick dismissals for Sarah Taylor and Heather Knight stunted any chances of the English winning. Nat Sciver-Brunt got the team scoring again with 19 runs on the board, meaning that with just a few more runs, England could draw level.

The result would be determined by the final ball of the contest, as Sciver-Brunt and Rebecca Grundy sealed the needed 109 runs right at the end of the match. The official result is listed as a one-wicket win, as England still had one left, but they would also have won by a single wicket. Both teams managed to qualify for the semi-finals from the group stage. Australia would knock England out in the semi-final... Meanwhile the West Indies went on to win the tournament. But at least England got this historic win!

THE FAMOUS TIED GAME IN BIRMINGHAM

England hosted the 1999 Cricket World Cup with venues all over the country. South Africa and Australia met in the semi-final in a match held at Edgbaston, Birmingham. The two teams had met in the Super Six phase at Headingley in Leeds, where Australia won by five wickets. The re-match, much deeper into the competition, was going to be another exciting fixture.

The Australians' batting efforts were very impressive, with Adam Gilchrist starting with 20 runs, only for Michael Bevan and Steve Waugh to score over 110. On the other side of the field, South Africa was also having a good time bowling. Shaun Pollock took five wickets in his overs, taking out the biggest Australian scorers. Allan Donald would later take four wickets in the match, leading to the end of the innings. Australia finished with 213 runs, around 60 runs short of what they'd managed in the last game against this team in the tournament.

South Africa knew that they could win this game with a good batting performance, having scored 271 in the Super Six phase. Herschelle Gibbs was a prominent scorer for South Africa but was sent off the field early with just 30 runs by an exceptional bowl from Shane Warne. The South African captain, Hanse Cronje, had an even worse afternoon. He was dismissed without making a run! Warne was having a great day bowling as he took four wickets in his overs, taking out some of the opponent's best players.

Jacques Kallis and Jonty Rhodes managed to get lots of runs on the board for South Africa. But the final over had Lance Klusener and Allan Donald out on the pitch against Australian bowler Damien Fleming. On the first ball, Klusener hit a boundary for four runs; now South Africa just needed another five to win the game and reach the World Cup final. The second ball was another boundary, and both teams were on 213 runs! A single run in the last four balls would have put South Africa into this final match.

The next key moment was in the fourth ball, where they still just needed a single run. Klusener hit the ball, but not perfectly. He went for a run; however, his partner, Donald, didn't see or hear the decision to make the run. Australia scrambled to dismiss Donald as he started to run very late, causing him to be run out. With both teams having ten dismissed and scoring 213 runs, they were level in all measures, and the match was officially ruled a draw. However, that didn't stop Australia from celebrating. As Australia had finished higher in the Super Six table earlier in the tournament, the rules stated that they would advance to the final because they had a better record in the competition. Australia advanced to the final against Pakistan at Lord's in London and went on to win the 1999 World Cup final by eight wickets.

CARIBBEAN CLASSIC IN BARBADOS

Since the Caribbean Premier League started in 2013, it has made some fantastic T20 cricket matches with its colourful and fast-paced approach to the game. One of the best games in the history of the competition was in 2015 at the Kensington Oval in Bridgetown, Barbados.

The Barbados Tridents were hosting the St Kitts & Nevis Patriots; interestingly, this was the visiting team's first season in the CPL. Joining at the start of 2015, this was only their second match ever! The Patriots batted first, sending legendary New Zealand player Martin Guptill to start the afternoon off. He and Evin Lewis managed to get the Patriots off to a good start, scoring over 40 runs between them. Rayad Emrit was in fine form bowling for the Tridents as he took two wickets to dismiss both Lewis and the Patriots captain, Marlon Samuels. Orlando Peters and Carlos Brathwaite managed to put more runs on the board, meaning that the Patriots set a score of 143 to beat if the Tridents wanted to win.

Sheldon Cottrell, who didn't bat especially well for the Patriots, was the first to step up to bowl. He made quick work for Dwayne Smith and Jonathan Carter. Shoaib Malik stepped up the performance with 35 runs for the Tridents, but that was nothing compared to what their captain was about to do. Kieron Pollard delivered a T20 masterpiece! His 82 runs from 58 balls put the Tridents right back in the game. Come the final ball, Pollard was standing with Navin Stewart. The Tridents needed two runs to force a super over or even more to win it. Coming off a Pollard boundary, there was excitement that they could do it. Stewart mis-hit the ball, Pollard was run out and the Tridents were out of time and left one run short, with 142. Pollard was named the man of the match, but he wasn't happy with the result.

This was St Kitts & Nevis Patriots' first-ever win. Unfortunately, the team would end up finishing last place (sixth out of six) in the league table. This win gave them some pride, however, though the Barbados Tridents finished the regular season as league leaders. They made it to the final but lost to the Trinbago Knight Riders.

CHARLOTTE EDWARDS AND KIM PRICE STEAL THE SHOW

Hyderabad is famous for great cricket, with many wonderful players coming from the city, and now for having the Hyderabad Sunrisers. However, in 1997, two players, neither from India, stole the show in the women's Cricket World Cup. The Group A fixture between England and South Africa was reduced to 20 overs each due to poor weather conditions, essentially making this ODI match a T20 game.

Not wanting to waste any time, Charlotte Edwards took the field immediately and scored 38 runs for England, eventually being stumped out by a ball bowled by Kim Price, the other woman who lit up this match. Price would take another wicket and generally make it hard for England to score runs. A late performance from Jane Smit and Kathryn Leng allowed England to finish the innings with 94 runs.

Despite swapping over, neither Edwards nor Price were finished, with both wanting to win. South Africa relied on Elizabeth Ackhurst and Kerri Lang to score many runs to help them chase down the runs needed. England's bowling lacked any real quality, with Sue Redfern having an off day. Toward the end of the overs, Kim Price picked up the bat and started to make lots of runs. By the end of the reduced overs, she had scored 15 from 12 balls. But these runs weren't enough, as Charlotte Edwards was taking out the South African batters with her expert bowling.

England won the game by seven runs, but the match was dominated by the two players, Edwards and Price, who performed at both ends of the pitch. Both teams qualified for the first knockout round, where South Africa was defeated by India. England made it to the semi-final but lost to New Zealand.

2019 WORLD CUP FINAL GOES TO A SUPER OVER

Sometimes, when a game is tied, the match result or prize for winning is given to the team with a better overall record in the tournament. Like the game in Birmingham (the last one), or if the series is drawn, the team that held the trophy before the series gets to keep it, because they didn't lose and the other team didn't win. Yet, sometimes, when the match is very important, the teams will play a Super Over. This is like extra time in football, where the teams will continue playing until one wins. That's exactly what happened in the 2019 World Cup Final between England and New Zealand.

England had reached their fourth World Cup final in this tournament, and the home crowd at Lord's wanted to see their team finally win the trophy. New Zealand batted first and initially struggled as England's Chris Woakes bowled out Martin Guptill with the leg-before-wicket rule. Woakes kept up this bowling performance as he took three wickets in his overs.

Henry Nicholls and Tom Latham made lots of runs for New Zealand. Liam Plunkett was very productive, bowling three wickets from his ten overs. New Zealand finished their innings, having scored 241 runs in a well-contested match.

The pressure was now on England to bat well if they were to win the Cricket World Cup for the first time. Some of their superstars failed to make an impact in the early going, as Joe Root was caught out with just seven runs, while captain Eoin Morgan only managed nine before being dismissed. Lockie

Ferguson had a terrific day for New Zealand, both bowling and catching English players out of the game.

But when England needed a hero, Ben Stokes entered the field of play and consistently chipped away at the lead with multiple runs. Jos Buttler also put in a great performance before being dismissed. Remarkably, at the end of 50 overs, both teams had 241 runs. This resulted in a Super Over being played.

Jos Buttler and the man of the hour, Ben Stokes, returned to the field of play for this additional period. The pair scored 15 runs from the Super Over without being dismissed, meaning that New Zealand needed 16 or more to win the World Cup. Jofra Archer took his place as the bowler for England, eager to stop the Kiwis from scoring. Martin Guptill and James Neesham started well to do this, scoring a maximum early on. The drama went down to the final delivery of the tournament. New Zealand needed two runs to win the championship. Guptill hit the ball in the middle of his bat; knowing he had to run, he moved but was too slow. Neesham made his run, but Guptill was run out, leaving the teams on 15 runs each from the Super Over.

The rules determined that if a Super Over is drawn, then a winner will be decided based on the amount of boundary scores they had throughout the entire match. Guptill was run out; the England fans, players and media knew this and were delighted knowing that they had 26 boundaries from the match compared to New Zealand's 17. Many of the players have since called this match the greatest cricket game of all time. The England team were given a hero's reception as they met with the British prime minister, Theresa May, to celebrate the World Cup win.

THREE RUNS SEPARATE 2023 ASHES CLASSIC

The Oval in London has held some exciting cricket matches in its long history, but a classic took place in 2023, with the second T20I match between the women's teams of England and Australia as part of the Ashes series. The matches before this one had been competitive, and fans of both nations thought they could win the series.

Sophia Dunkley and Danni Wyatt started the batting for England in great style. Wyatt managed to score 76 runs from 46 balls. Annabel Sutherland got three wickets for the Australian bowling efforts, but the English were still able to get 186 runs after the 20 overs.

When Australia took to the field to bat, they started with Alyssa Healey, the captain, and Beth Mooney. The pairing scored 59 runs between them from very few balls as they looked to chase the runs made by the English. Sarah Glenn, Nat Sciver-Brunt and Sophie Ecclestone had other ideas, though. Their bowling performances allowed very few runs for the Australians; however, they were getting closer and closer. At the end of 20 overs, Australia only had 183 runs, falling short by three.

England had won that T20I match, yet the overall series was drawn. Australia retained the Ashes because they hadn't technically lost. Nat Sciver-Brunt was named the player of the series, and there was no doubt that the English were now at the same level as Australia, the nation that had dominated women's cricket until then.

IPL SHOWDOWN IN 2014

The Indian Premier League is, for many T20 cricket fans, the best place for T20 cricket. In 2014, the Rajasthan Royals and the

Mumbai Indians put on one of the best matches in the history of the competition.

The Rajasthan Royals batted first and started with Sanju Samson, who put together a 74 score from just 47 balls. While Shane Watson, the captain, was dismissed early, he was replaced by Karun Nair, who scored another 50 for the Royals. Brad Hodge was in the midst of a great run with 29 runs from only 16 balls when the overs finished, leaving the Royals with 189 runs.

When the teams switched over, Lendl Simmons and Michael Hussey started the batting efforts for the Mumbai Indians. However, it was Corey Anderson who made the difference for the team. He came on and made runs at an astounding rate, finishing the game not out with 95 runs from 44 balls. Amazingly, he did this while established cricket superstars like Rohit Sharma (the club captain) and Kieron Pollard had poor performances, scoring very few runs.

By the end of the overs, Anderson was standing with Aditya Tare, who hit a maximum from the one ball he faced. This was enough for the Mumbai Indians to win the match. At the end of the regular season, this win was enough to separate the teams in the league table, allowing Mumbai Indians to play in the post-season while the Rajasthan Royals did not qualify, since they were in fifth place.

1986 CLASSIC BETWEEN BITTER RIVALS

Many years ago, the 1986 Austral-Asia Cup took place with teams representing nations from Australasia and Asia in the UAE. India and Pakistan emerged as the best two teams in the competition by reaching the final. These long-standing cricket rivals produced one of the best-ever cricket matches, which people still talk about with great excitement.

India batted first and started with their best three players. Krishnamachari Srikkanth made 75 runs, Sunil Gavaskar followed that up with 92, while another 50 were made by Dilip Vengsarkar. Unfortunately for them, Pakistan were eventually able to dismiss them and quickly get through to the other players. Imran Khan and Wasim Akram bowled 20 excellent overs between them and managed to earn five wickets. India ended their innings with 245 runs, a decent score, but Pakistan knew they had stunted their opponent's score with some heroic bowling.

The batting for Pakistan started slowly, with Mudassar Nazar and Rameez Raja both being bowled out quickly. The game changed pace when Javed Miandad entered the field to bat. He would consistently score runs, and the opposition couldn't seem to dismiss him. The Indian bowlers couldn't limit or match the performance of their rivals, as Kapil Dev didn't look like his usual self in this game. Yet others on the Indian team were able to limit Pakistan from scoring as much.

Come the final delivery, Mohammad Azharuddin was bowling for India. Pakistan needed four runs and a wicket to win the game. Remarkably, Javed Miandad, who was not out, hit a maximum at this point to wrap up the game and championship. Miandad took his score to 116 runs and was named Player of the Match as Pakistan lifted the 1986 Austral-Asia Cup.

TRENT ROCKETS WIN BY THREE RUNS IN THE HUNDRED

The summer British cricket season has been radically changed by the advent of the new The Hundred competition. In the 2023 regular season, the women's teams of the Trent Rockets and the Birmingham Phoenix put on a limited-balls clinic.

Trent Rockets were led by Bryony Smith, who scored 64 runs in just 40 balls! Nat Sciver-Brunt also played quite well, along with other players like Harmanpreet Kaur and Fran Wilson. Emily Arlott was in good form for the Phoenix and took three wickets in the process. By the end of the 100 balls, the Trent Rockets had scored 134 runs.

When the teams switched around, the Phoenix started very brightly. Sophie Devine made 28 runs before Amy Jones got 46 for the team, which put the Phoenix back in contention for winning the match. A little lull followed, which slowed them in meeting the Rockets' run score. Emily Arlott hit a maximum as she scored nine runs in just three balls. She was run out, and the balls simply ran out before they could score any more runs. In the end, they would finish on 131 runs, giving the Trent Rockets a win by just three runs.

Unfortunately, both teams finished outside the top three places in the league table, so neither advanced to the next stage of the competition.

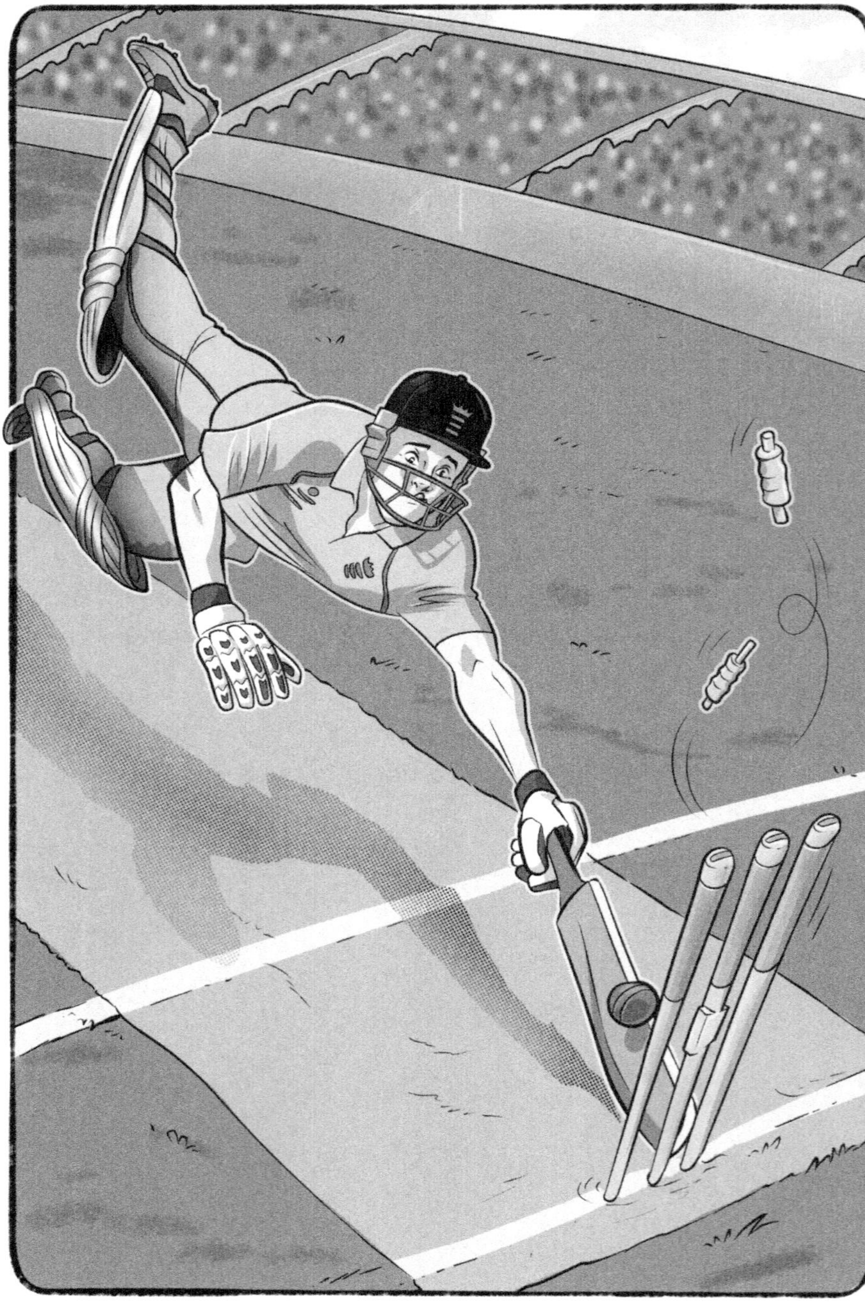

5

INCREDIBLE FACTS ABOUT CRICKET

Here are some very interesting facts about cricket that you can use to impress your friends and family.

1. The Cricket World Cup 2007 was the 'biggest' edition of the competition, with 16 teams participating in that event. Since then, the number of teams playing in the event has been reduced.

2. Cricket was played at the 1900 Olympics in Paris. Great Britain took home the gold medal!

3. Since then, cricket has not been played at the Olympic Games, but it is scheduled to be back in the games for the 2028 edition in Los Angeles.

4. Denmark's women's cricket team have played in two World Cups, but the men's team hasn't played in any.

5. The United States will play in their first T20 World Cup in 2024, when they co-host the tournament with the West Indies.

6. Mahendra Singh Dhoni is an incredible player for India, but he has never scored a century outside of Asia.

7. The fastest-ever bowled ball was made by Shoaib Akhtar while he was playing for Pakistan against England in 2003. The speed of the bowl was reported to be over 100mph!

8. Sachin Tendulkar has the most runs across all disciplines of cricket, having scored more than 34,000 in over 660 matches!

9. Yorkshire Cricket Club has won the highest number of County Championships in England, with 33 titles.

10. The Australian women's team have played 84 matches at the Cricket World Cup and won 70 of them.

11. The Deccan Chargers won the Indian Premier League in 2009 but then stopped playing in 2012. They were replaced by Sunrisers Hyderabad.

12. Games played in The Hundred competition often come in pairs, with both men's and women's teams playing on the same day.

13. The fourth Test match between England and Australia in the 2013-14 series recorded one of the largest attendances ever, with 91,112 people watching the match at Melbourne Cricket Ground.

14. The Cricket World Cup will return to Africa in 2027 when the tournament is co-hosted by South Africa, Zimbabwe and Namibia.

15. The United States is actively seeing more people to become interested in cricket, with the introduction of Major League Cricket.

16. Because Test matches and ODI cricket can take all day, it is not uncommon for the games to break for lunch. Older cricket fans and some players will often have jam sandwiches.

17. Ash Barty is well known for being a top tennis player, but she's also very good at cricket, playing for both Brisbane Heat and Queensland.

18. Players don't normally change nationality in cricket, but Iftikhar Ali Khan Pataudi first played for England and then switched to play for India.

19. In 2019, the Blunham Cricket Club in Bedfordshire, England set the world record for playing cricket for the longest time continuously. They played for 168 hours and 20 minutes. That's a whole week of cricket!

20. The biggest cricket ground in the world is the Narendra Modi Stadium in Gujarat, India.

AFTERWORD

Congratulations! You've now journeyed through the grand stadiums, grassy fields, and thrilling moments that make up the world of cricket. From discovering the origins of this historic game to learning about the legends who have shaped it, you've gathered a treasure trove of cricket knowledge. And remember those tricky rules and cricket terms? Now you're tossing them around like a pro!

But don't let your adventure stop here. Cricket is a game best enjoyed not just through stories and facts, but by experiencing the excitement yourself. Watching a cricket match on TV is a great way to see the action up close. You can observe how players strategize and react in real-time, and maybe you'll even predict what they'll do next!

If you get a chance, nothing beats the thrill of watching a cricket match in person. The energy of the crowd, the sound of the ball hitting the bat, and the cheer that erupts with every run scored is something truly magical. It's a wonderful way to feel connected to the millions of cricket fans around the world.

AFTERWORD

And why stop at watching? Cricket is a game for everyone, and there are plenty of ways you can start playing. Whether joining a local team, playing with friends in a park, or even practicing your batting and bowling in your backyard, every moment you spend playing brings you closer to becoming a part of the cricket community.

As you continue to watch, play, and enjoy cricket, you'll make new friends, learn new skills, and become part of exciting matches that you'll remember for a lifetime. So, keep your cricket bat handy and your passion for the game alive. Who knows? Maybe one day, you'll be the cricket hero inspiring young fans, just like the legends you've read about in this book.

Ready to step out and play? The field is waiting, and the game is just beginning. Here's to your cricket journey—may it be as exciting and rewarding as a perfectly played game!

Printed in Great Britain
by Amazon